PAUL H. NITZE ON FOREIGN POLICY

Volume XIII

W. Alton Jones Foundation Series on Arms Control

**Edited by Kenneth W. Thompson
and Steven L. Rearden**

UNIVERSITY
PRESS OF
AMERICA

Lanham • New York • London

The Miller Center

University of Virginia

Copyright © 1989 by

University Press of America,® Inc.

4720 Boston Way
Lanham, MD 20706

3 Henrietta Street
London WC2E 8LU England

Printed in the United States of America

British Cataloging in Publication Information Available

ISBN 0–8191–7615–X (alk. paper)
ISBN 0–8191–7616–8 (pbk. : alk. paper)

Co-published by arrangement with
The White Burkett Miller Center of Public Affairs,
University of Virginia

The paper used in this publication meets the minimum requirements of American
National Standard for Information Sciences—Permanence of Paper for Printed Library
Materials, ANSI Z39.48–1984.   ∞

TO

CHARLES BURTON MARSHALL

AND

JOHN COURTNEY MURRAY, S.J.

Acknowledgements

Our special thanks are due Mrs. Pat Dunn, publication director of the Miller Center, who organized the editing and preparation of the manuscript, and typed the final text. We also wish to thank Mr. Steven L. Rearden, who is responsible for most of the editorial material in the volume. Finally, Mr. Nitze's longtime administrative assistant, Ann M. Smith, deserves warm thanks for all her faithful service to him and to the Miller Center.

Table of Contents

TABLE OF CONTENTS

Preface

The distinguished *New York Times* columnist James Reston has observed that few if any Americans have served their government with greater distinction over a longer period of time than Paul H. Nitze. Less well known is the contribution Mr. Nitze has made to higher education and scholarship. In the late 1950s, he established the Washington Center for American Foreign Policy Research. Earlier he was a founding father along with Christian Herter, Massachusetts congressman and later secretary of state, of the Johns Hopkins University School for Advanced International Studies in Washington. At these and other institutions, he encouraged countless emerging scholars and young policy-makers and helped them in launching their careers.

Mr. Nitze's career is in effect a chronicle of wartime and postwar America. In 1941, he left Dillon Read to join the Office of the Coordinator of Inter-American Affairs. During World War II, he served on the Board of Economic Warfare and the Foreign Economic Administration. He received the Medal of Merit for his work as vice chairman of the United States Strategic Bombing Survey. For seven years he held important positions in the Department of State culminating in his appointment in 1950 as director of the Policy Planning Staff succeeding George Kennan.

When President Kennedy took office in 1961, Mr. Nitze became assistant secretary of defense and in 1963 secretary of the navy. In 1967, President Johnson named him to be deputy secretary of defense. From the spring of 1969 to the summer of 1974, he represented the secretary of defense on the U.S. Delegation to the Strategic Arms Limitation Talks with the Soviet Union. Beginning on November 30, 1981, he headed the U.S. Delegation to the Intermediate-Range Nuclear Force Negotiations with the Soviet Union.

From December 5, 1984, to the end of the Reagan administration, he served as a special adviser to the President and secretary of state on arms control matters.

It seems fitting, therefore, to bring together in two volumes some of Mr. Nitze's most important papers on foreign policy and national security and arms control. Mr. Steven L. Rearden has devoted himself over the years to the collection and classification of Mr. Nitze's essays, articles, speeches, correspondence, and public papers. As editor of a Miller Center of Public Affairs series on foreign policy and arms control and as a long-time friend of Paul Nitze, I have undertaken to bring this publication within the framework of the Center's program. Having assisted Mr. Nitze in the creation of the Washington Center, I am honored to continue that relationship in making available his papers to a wider public than may have read them in their original form.

CHAPTER I:

Theory and Practice

CHAPTER I: THEORY AND PRACTICE

Introduction

For a dozen years from 1940, Paul Nitze dealt with the practical problems of a government engaged in fighting a great war and then in molding a postwar world. In 1953, after being forced to leave public service, he moved his office to the School of Advanced International Studies in Washington, D.C. In that environment he had the time and stimulus to seek out general principles that might give form, structure, and greater clarity to the mass of detail involved in the practical conduct of politics and government.

The ideas that he developed there on the relationship between theory and practice had their origins, in part, in ideas that had influenced him in his years at school and at Harvard College, and in part, also, in the ideas he had developed while working in government. They were refined in greater detail and with greater rigor during the seven years between his departure from office in 1953 and his return to full-time concern with the actual conduct of governmental affairs at the end of 1960.

The papers in this chapter thus differ from those that follow in that they all derive from a rather limited time span—the 1950s. Having been written around the same time, they have much in common and, taken as a whole, effectively capture the essence of Nitze's "philosophy" of foreign affairs and national security. His outlook is more that of a practitioner than a theoretician; and, as evidence of this, he draws heavily on his experiences to illustrate or support his arguments. Even so, Mr. Nitze holds to the belief, reiterated throughout these papers, that a successful and credible foreign policy requires a solid conceptual basis that presupposes what that policy should strive to achieve and how that policy ought to be conducted.

1. Groton Commencement Address*

(1953)

Sixth Form of 1953, I salute you, praise you, and wish you well.

In times to come you will look back on these years at Groton with deepening appreciation. These were the formative years—the years when you absorbed even more than you realized at the time, when you rejected certain things, when you grew, developed form, each one different, an individual but bound by common loyalties, common memories, and as yet vague but growing aspirations for the future.

*This paper is the commencement address that Nitze delivered in June 1953 at Groton School, where his son, Peter, was a member of the graduating class. Nitze says he can recall no speech to the preparing of which he devoted more effort. He remembered his own days at Hotchkiss and the cruelty with which he and some of his classmates had treated one of their number whose uncle was the Episcopal Bishop of Connecticut and had delivered a sermon one Sunday which they found particularly boring. Nitze was determined not to cause similar embarrassment to his son. It was also his view that boys of sixteen had penetrating minds. They could distinguish cant from wisdom better than most adults. Therefore one should not talk down to them or use cliches; rather, one should speak to them honestly and in clear language. Nitze continues to believe that the ideas contained in that speech are basic to an understanding of his own thinking.

5

Before speaking of that future, I should like to go back for a minute to the past.

On the day of my graduation from Hotchkiss twenty-nine years ago today, the things in the forefront of mind were whether I was really going to get to Europe that summer, whether I had been right in deciding to go to Harvard rather than to Yale, and particularly whether the plus fours I had acquired from J. Press, the New Haven tailor, really hung down close enough to my ankles in the style of those years.

In the back of my mind, however, there lay an uneasiness about life with a capital L. It seemed to me that the great creative ages, as one read about them in the history books, were Greece in the days of Pericles, the Italian city states in the days of the Medici, the United States in the days of Adams, of Jefferson, and of Hamilton. Somehow it was difficult to see the life opening up before us in the 1920s as being related to that history, to the potential greatness and creativeness of man, to something that would make it worthwhile, or even possibly, to be very concrete about aspirations much beyond Mr. Press's plus fours or, perhaps, his white flannels with 20 inch cuffs.

As the years passed, two things became clear. The first was that history was not something just of the past; it was something very much of the present and of the future. It was something that almost seemed to have an independent life and force of its own; something that could catch up a sleep-walking world and shake it into wakefulness. Maybe the era of the 1920s, the 1930s, and the 1940s was not Greece of the age of Pericles; maybe it was not Florence of the Medici, or the United States of Adams. But it was the 1920s, the 1930s, the 1940s of the United States, and it did matter whether that era moved in one direction or in another direction.

The second thing that became clear was that people were being caught up in the stream of events, were assuming responsibility, and that the character of those who were assuming responsibility impinged upon the stream of life and of history and was in turn reinforced and strengthened by those streams.

Among those who were acting with a sense of responsibility, a disproportionately large number were Groton men. Those men seemed to combine two concurrent qualities. One was a deep understanding of history, of principle, of character—qualities generally associated with a conservative point of view. The other quality was that of not only accepting the necessity for change and adaptation, but indeed welcoming and working for change, development, and growth—qualities generally associated with a liberal point of view.

This unity of apparent opposites seems to me to involve a basic and crucial point. Twenty-five hundred years ago Heraclitus, using the analogies of the bow and of the lyre, suggested that harmony and truth were to be found in the tension of opposites. Today advanced modern scientists, such as Robert Oppenheimer and Niels Bohr, apply a parallel idea. They tell us that the basic truths in their field can be attained only by the concurrent application of complementary ideas which to our senses seem contradictory—as for example, we can understand the behavior of light only by perceiving it in two opposite concepts—that of the wave and that of the particle. They call this the principle of complementarity.

Heraclitus and the atomic scientists go on to suggest that this principle of the complementarity of opposites applies not only to the world of physics, but generally, including the world of human affairs.

The great problems with which all of us have been wrestling, and with which each of you will be called upon to wrestle in very concrete terms, include the individual versus society, change versus continuing order, force versus consent, the East versus the West, power versus responsibility. In each case it would seem to me that the answer is not to be found in the elimination of one of the opposites or in any basic compromise between them but in striving for a harmony in the tension between the opposites.

It is the province of a commencement speaker to give advice. I offer the following.

The first is to strive for both the general and the concrete. Some men combine in themselves a general wisdom derived from a deep background in the humanities and the general sciences with an ability to deal responsibly with particulars. Such men retain breadth of vision with a sense of care for relevant details. They make a wholly disproportionate contribution in the world of affairs. Again it is not a compromise between the general and the concrete which I am advocating. In the field of foreign affairs for instance, it is not those who have taken specialized courses in international affairs who make the real contribution; it is those who combine a truly humanistic background with a sense for relevant facts and an intense care for the significant details who are invaluable.

My second bit of advice would be to head into problems rather than away from them. If one heads into problems, if one addresses oneself to solving problems rather than fighting the fact that there is a problem, if one finds at an early age opportunities to assume responsibilities, then all manner of opportunities open out before one for satisfying service. In order to be able to carry responsibility in important matters, it is essential to have gained experience through trial and error in handling responsibility in smaller matters. It is only after one has survived and overcome a number of failures that one develops the stamina and courage to become a participant and molder of history—not merely an object of history.

My third bit of advice deals with the opposites of humility and of pride. I would apply the advice of Heraclitus and of the modern scientists to these opposites. Both are essential—humility before God, before nature, before mankind; pride in one's faith, in one's country and in one's association with one's fellow man. Only with humility can men gain wisdom and a true sense of relationship with God and with mankind. But only with a due sense of pride in oneself, in one's background and in one's country can one act with courage and effectiveness.

As to yourselves, I know many of you and have seen something of your growth and development. I know you can take pride in yourselves.

As to your background, including the background of Groton, you can take justified pride in that.

The crucial questions arise with respect to the United States and its position in the world and its relation to history.

The fact that the United States finds itself with increased power and responsibility but with less freedom of action than in years past gives us all a certain sense of uneasiness and frustration. We are going through a period of significant transition that is difficult and upsetting and which leads to a search for scapegoats and to mutual recrimination. It is easy enough to tear down and to cast blame. It is much more difficult to address oneself to the problem with cool nerves and a realistic eye.

Prior to the war we felt that there was a rough balance of power in the world outside this hemisphere. We could sit back behind the Atlantic and Pacific Oceans and only throw our weight into affairs beyond this hemisphere at crucial moments. When we did so it was with enormous effectiveness, as the situation without our intervention had been in close balance.

With the destruction of German and Japanese power, the weakening of the British and French Empires, and the great increase in the power of the U.S.S.R., all this has changed. Today no alliance strong enough to stand up against the Kremlin is possible without a strong United States. We can no longer choose when to throw in our influence. Our influence is continually necessary. This makes us feel that our freedom of action has been restricted.

This, coupled with the ruthless and implacable hostility of the U.S.S.R. and the range and power of modern weapons, has radically altered the situation of this country and of all of its citizens. We now find ourselves living in a situation of continuing threat and tension comparable to that in which most of the other great powers of history continually lived.

Future historians may well judge that the United States moved toward a preliminary adjustment to this new situation with remarkable speed and adaptability; and that it made this preliminary adjustment in a manner consistent with its basic principles.

A more radical test, both of our stamina and of our capabilities for growth and development in character and in accomplishment opens up before us. The process will be long and difficult. It will involve much new and intense thought. Some of the old structure which shielded us from the necessity of looking whole-eyed and whole-mindedly at the truth will have fallen away. That independence of thought combined with a sense of responsibility for which Groton graduates have been renowned throughout the world will be needed to the full. Opening up before us, particularly before you, the oncoming generation, one can see a vital era—an era in the main stream of history—an opportunity to participate in the growth of the human spirit.

To the Sixth Form of 1953, Godspeed for the journey.

2. The Role of the Learned Man in Government*

(1958)

In the context of government, what do we mean by the phrase "a learned man"? I take it we can mean a variety of things.

On the one hand, we can have in mind the specialist, the expert, the man with an intensive and specialized background in a particular field of knowledge. On the other hand, we can have in mind the man with general wisdom, with that feeling for the past and the future which

*In this selection, adapted from a 1958 speech to the Catholic Commission on Intellectual and Cultural Affairs, Nitze turns his attention to the ever-present need for able and effective public servants, especially in the increasingly important fields of foreign affairs and national security. In part, the paper is a rebuttal to the strong current of anti-intellectualism that made itself felt in the 1950s. But it is something more—a reaffirmation of the idea that intellectual creativity is as important to the functioning of government as it is to other walks of life. With this in mind, Nitze draws a distinction between the expert, or specialist, who may be exceptionally well-informed on a particular subject, and someone whose interests and capabilities are on a broader plain. As indispensable as the expert may be, Nitze contends that the "learned man, the man of general wisdom and with a taste for politics," has an equally significant and unique contribution to make.

enriches a sense for the present, and with that appreciation for wider loyalties which deepens patriotism to one's country and finds bonds between it and Western culture and links with the universal aspirations of mankind.

And when we refer to such a learned man—whether the expert or the man of generalized wisdom—in government, we can think of him in various roles. We can think of him as an adviser. We can think of him as a responsible official politically accountable for his actions. We can think of him in one or the other branch of government, in the judiciary, in the legislature, or in the executive. And if he is in the executive branch we can think of him as a diplomat, a soldier, a civil servant with general administrative duties, or as an elected or politically appointed official with full political accountability.

Now what are the issues which arise with respect to the learned man in government? I propose to discuss two of them. The first question is that of the desirability of having learned men in government. In what circumstances can they play a useful role? In what circumstances are they inadequate or misplaced?

The second and directly related question is that of the special privileges or exemptions which it is advisable or inadvisable to give to the learned man to get the most out of what he has to contribute and to protect him from direct political assault.

These are issues which are not often objectively debated. Generally the issue gets itself posed in excessively simple terms as a polemic for or against egg-heads. In academic circles and in most of the responsible press, the usual position is that all men good and true should fight against the anti-intellectual currents of our time and protect the man of learning from the vulgar pressures of public opinion and the corrupting influences of politics. I propose that there is more to the issue than that.

Let us deal first with the question of the expert. There can be no doubt that in a business as complex as that of government in today's world the expert is indispensable. No one would think of conducting government today without the service of expert specialists in everything from accounting, agronomy, astronomy, and ballistics through the alphabet to experts in the making of wood pulp and in the care and feeding of zebras.

During the war I was for a time in charge of the overseas development and procurement of strategic materials for the war production effort. We had a team of some thousand geologists, mining engineers; experts in the growing of rubber, of sisal, and of chinchona bark; and specialists in the procurement of what were called casings but were really sheep guts, dried Mexican prairie bones to be used in the manufacture of glue, pig bristles for paint brushes, and even dried cuttlefish bones for the grinding of precision lenses. The political ideas or policy orientation of such experts, when functioning in the government solely as experts, is of secondary importance. Their role is to give specialized advice on technical matters of fact. Their primary function does not include providing the answer to important "should" propositions—to propositions of political policy.

It happens that almost all mining engineers are not only Republicans but tend to be on the conservative side of Republican politics. I rather suspect that this comes about because, in so speculative a business as that of finding and developing underground mineral resources, there is a very real need for careful and conservative patterns of action. In any case, almost all the mining engineers engaged in strategic materials work during the war were Republicans. Our immediate boss during those years was Vice President Henry Wallace who was then far over on the left wing of the Democratic party. He was somewhat worried about the politically conservative views of his mining engineers and they were somewhat concerned by what they considered to be their boss's radical political position. But the technical work went on with no real friction. Both sides agreed that there was a war to be won and that expert technical work could help win it.

Subsequently, in the 1949-1950 period, a more serious issue arose over the testing of a thermonuclear weapon. Dr. Oppenheimer was chairman of the General Advisory Committee to the Atomic Energy Commission and also served from time to time as a consultant to the State Department. When the question arose as to whether or not to proceed with a test of a thermonuclear weapon, it was our view in the State Department that Dr. Robert Oppenheimer was to be considered an expert on scientific matters, not an expert on political or military matters. We sought and used his advice on judgments of scientific fact. We had no scruple whatsoever in ignoring his views on general policy. We saw no reason why he should not have views on political matters. Every expert, in addition to being an expert in his particular field, is as entitled to political views as any other citizen. But, as we saw it, specialized knowledge in one field does not lead to a presumption of superior wisdom in all other fields. Furthermore, the responsibility for the political decisions involved in proceeding or not proceeding with a thermonuclear test was that of the president, advised by his secretaries of state and defense, and not the responsibility of Oppenheimer or any committee of atomic scientists. Mr. Acheson disagreed with Dr. Oppenheimer's political judgments and recommended a course of action to the President contrary to the one recommended by the scientists. It never occurred to us, however, to be annoyed by Dr. Oppenheimer's political views or to think that he should be penalized for them. In our view his responsibilities did not include political judgments of the kind involved in that particular decision. Inasmuch as we did not propose to be guided by his political views we felt we could avail ourselves of his undoubted scientific *expertise* while ignoring those of his recommendations which seemed to be based on political rather than scientific considerations.

The point about the expert is that the politically important decisions should be, and generally are, taken with the technical advice of experts, where technical matters are significant factors, but on the authority and final judgment of men with political responsibility. And success in carrying political responsibility usually calls for general wisdom more than it calls for specialized knowledge. Specialized knowledge and general wisdom are not necessarily in conflict. They are, however, not the same thing; and are not always to be found together in the same man.

Our analysis has now brought us around to a consideration of the role of the man of general wisdom in government and his relationship to political responsibility.

First, let me say a few words in comment on the distinctive contribution which the learned man of general wisdom can bring to government. In the introductory paragraph to this paper I suggested three aspects of that contribution. The first aspect is suggested by the word "general," a willingness and an ability to concern himself with the full range of implications and considerations which bear on a decision.

A second quality of the learned man is that of being able to relate the past and the future to the present—the ability, on the one hand, to tap the wisdom of the past and give it continuity into the present, and, on the other hand, to sense the possibilities and the needs of the future as they emerge from the developing present. Perhaps this quality is more directly associable with outstanding leadership, the leadership of a Churchill or a Lincoln, than with learning as such. I prefer to think, however, that it is not unconnected with humanistic learning, particularly with care for and understanding of history.

A third quality associated with the learned man of general wisdom is that appreciation for wider loyalties which deepens patriotism to one's country and finds bonds between it and Western culture and links with the universal aspirations of mankind. I am reminded of a marginal note in one of the books in John Adams' library in which he asks himself the following question: "In truth what is comprehended in the spirit of patriotism?" He answers: "Piety, or the love and fear of God; general benevolence to mankind; a particular attachment to our own country; a zeal to promote its happiness by reforming its morals, increasing its knowledge, promoting its agriculture, commerce and manufactures, improving its constitution, and securing its liberties; and all this without the prejudices of individuals or parties or factions, without fear, favor, or affection." Not only do men exist in our government who have precisely the zeal that John Adams described but they are reasonably numerous. They constitute the hard core of that selfless band of civil servants without whom the great and constructive projects carried forward by our government since the war could not have been executed. They have, when not suppressed by more narrowly chauvinistic elements, given to our policy a breadth and a humanity the effects of which have even yet not been entirely lost.

But, if so many good things can be said about the learned man, the man of general wisdom, in government, why is there an issue? Why can't one take the simple course of saying all power to the egg-heads, down with the anti-intellectuals? Why should we have certain reservations?

I think the answer is to be found in two related circumstances. The first is that the learned man, or at least the man whose orientation is primarily analytical or academic, finds it difficult to act resolutely within the limits prescribed by the real situation with which, in the realm of government, he is always faced, and finding it difficult he tends to have a distaste for full political responsibility. The second circumstance is that, not desiring to accept full political responsibility, he nevertheless strives for a free and controlling hand in the guidance of those matters on which his interest focuses. The result is a tendency toward separating responsibility from power, and power from responsibility.

Let us expand somewhat upon these thoughts. I take it that the analytic and academic approach to policy problems is apt to exhibit two tendencies: the first is a tendency toward abstraction and generalization; the second is a tendency to emphasize historical analogies. These tendencies have their virtues but also have shortcomings which are the obverse of those virtues.

I recall Mr. Acheson's instructions to us in the days when George Kennan, and then I, were directing the Policy Planning job in the State Department. Mr. Acheson said he wanted from us continuous and forthright advice as to the courses of United States governmental action in international affairs which in our judgment would best serve the interests of the United States without regard to the domestic acceptability of those courses of action or the feasibility of securing congressional support for them. He said that Mr. Truman, with his, Mr. Acheson's, advice and that of others whose judgment he respected, would take the responsibility for adjusting, modifying, and compromising the suggested courses of action to bring them into accord with the realities of the domestic political scene. But he and Mr. Truman did not want that job done twice. They did not want a recommended course of action to be watered down because of domestic political considerations at several different levels. They wanted to have a clear idea themselves as to what compromises were being made and for what reasons. The staff work which we undertook was therefore abstracted from the reality of the political scene by the elimination of one important category of real consideration—domestic political factors. Even within the remaining field the use of simplifying generalizations and abstractions was necessary in order to compress the vast complex of relevant data into a manageable analytic framework. Generalization is necessary and useful. Without it staff work cannot be done. But its product is essentially staff work. The final decision must be taken by someone prepared to take all the real factors into consideration and to breathe completeness and life back into otherwise arid analytic generalizations.

Similar considerations apply to the tendency of academically oriented advisers to hark back to the analogies of history. Historical analogies have great utility in illuminating complex situations and in helping one to sort out the significant from the merely striking. But action based too closely on historical analogies is apt to be sterile and unimaginative.

The other day I came across a passage in Maurice Paléologue's memoirs in which he quotes a comment Delcassé, the French foreign minister, made to him in 1904. Paléologue had just read him a passage from a Polish student of Russian history who drew an analogy between recurrent Russian behavior and that of an avalanche. Delcassé snapped back at him:

"Why do you make me read such stuff? . . . You know I don't consider history of any practical use. . . . All historians are false guides because they are out of touch with reality, or rather, because they see it *a posteriori*, in retrospect, after events have happened and it is no longer possible to change their course. . . . It is just the opposite for the statesman: he sees events *on their way*, with all the risks, openings, possibilities and opportunities for skillful handling which they offer. . . . Can you see me consulting a history book in a crisis? Not I! At such moments what counts most is flair, a cool head, courage, resolution and nimble wits. . . . Beware of history, my dear Paléologue!"

Paléologue, however, concluded his report of Delcassé's reaction with the following comments:

"All the same, Waliszewski's ominous prediction seemed to have got home; twice did he mutter in gloomy tones: *Beware of the avalanche! . . . Beware of the avalanche!* Then with an irritable frown, he turned to the business of the day."[1]

I can remember occasions on which Mr. Acheson was similarly dubious as to the help which more academically or

---

[1]*Three Critical Years: 1904-05-06* (New York, 1957), p. 59.

analytically minded men could give him in enabling him better to handle the very real and concrete problems and opportunities which faced him. It is reported that today Mr. Dulles says that he would welcome assistance from those who have more knowledge of and experience with the foreign policy problems which the world now faces than he has, but he asks where are there such people.

We are faced then with a possible gulf between the learned expert and the man carrying political responsibility. George Kennan has given expression to the effect which this gulf can have upon the point of view of a trained diplomat. In a paper[2] presented before the American Historical Association in December, 1955, he compares the trained diplomat to a mechanic condemned to tinker with a badly designed car or to a physician with a shabby and irritating group of patients. He will go on treating them as long as he is permitted to, saving them from such of their follies as he can, patching up the damages done by those follies from which he cannot save them.

Kennan further comments that the professional sees the relations between governments as largely the product of the follies and ambitions and brutalities of that minority of the human race which is always attracted by the possibility of exercising power over the remainder of it, in whatever political framework the age provides. He sees the task of the trained diplomat as essentially that of hovering around the fringes of a process he is powerless to control and of which he deeply disapproves. The picture that he paints of the professional is that of a hopeless man dedicated to a menial task.

Contrast this with the picture given by Mr. Acheson in a letter discussing the reasons why young men might be encouraged to choose a career in government service.

"And yet I would be eager to see them [young, and, also, old men of quality] steered toward a career, perhaps a life, of public service, as some of their ancestors were. Why? Not because I see the gleam of a halo forming about their heads, . . . but because there is no better or fuller life for a man of spirit. The old Greek conception of

---

[2]Printed in *The Review of Politics*, XVIII (April, 1956), pp. 170-177.

happiness is relevant here: 'The exercise of vital powers along lines of excellence, in a life affording them scope'.

"This is the geiger-counter which tells where to dig. It explains why to everyone who has ever experienced it the return from public life to private life leaves one feeling flat and empty. Contented, interested, busy—yes. But exhilarated—no. For one has left a life affording scope for the exercise of vital powers along lines of excellence. Not the only one, I am sure. Undoubtedly Einstein, Michaelangelo, Savonarola, Shakespeare, and others could give testimony on other lives. But outside of aesthetics and teaching—religion belongs to both—the requirement of 'scope' is hard to come by in this age, outside of public life. . . . It gives a feeling of zest, a sense that the only limitation upon the exercise of all one's vital powers is one's capacity. . . .

" . . . Today, more than ever before, the prize of the general is not a bigger tent, but command. The managers of industry and finance have the bigger tents; but command rests with government. Command, or, if one prefers, supreme leadership, demands and gives scope for the exercise of every vital power a man has in the direction of excellence.

"How, then, does one present to the youth a life of public service? Not, I am sure, as an evangelist appealing to the young squires to turn their backs on the world and dedicate themselves to a secular order for ministering to the peasants. . . . Rather, I think, one educates them to know the world in which they live, to understand that government will go on whether they take part in it or not, that command is too important to be entrusted to the ignorant, even though they may be well meaning and dedicated, and to an understanding of the good life, of happiness as the Greeks saw it, of the joy of exercising vital powers in a life affording them scope, of the limitless scope of governmental responsibilities. In addition, they might learn, as an authority on the process of revolution has pointed out, that 'Brave men are not uncommon in any system, but there is a tendency in most systems to make courage and a disciplined openness of mind to the significant facts mutually exclusive. This is the immediate cause of the downfall of every ruling class that ever falls.'"[3]

Here we have two points of view. The one looks upon the politically responsible process as being largely reserved to the follies of the ambitious and the brutal. The other looks upon the politically responsible process as being the arena in which human excellence can have scope for its full development.

In part these contrasting views reflect differences in the character of the two men. They, also, derive from differences in temperament, sensibility, and outlook. What to one is an opportunity for the display of courage and excellence, oppresses the other as being tainted with ambition and brutality. A task which one welcomes as offering a personal opportunity, the other looks upon as a duty which he must perform despite his distaste for it.

But over and beyond these indications of a difference in character is a difference in the situation in which they found themselves, the roles which they were called upon to fill in government. One was secretary of state under a president whose complete confidence he enjoyed. He was, thus, able to play a full political role with the essential elements of command. The other functioned as a staff officer called upon for specialized knowledge and advice in a limited though vital field—the power of decision being reserved to others.

The relationship between the specialist and the responsible wielders of political authority in government is always somewhat awkward. The specialist is asked to keep his eyes focused on fact, to avert them from partisanship, special interest, and immediate political pressures. The wielder of political authority must somehow deal with, compromise, and manage just these interests and pressures and do so from a position of party responsibility. Various techniques must therefore be worked out to enable each group to relate itself to the others.

In the judicial branch of the government we feel the need for men of general wisdom who will take into consideration the wider implications of their decisions but who are insulated from the full heat of the immediate

---

[3]This letter was quoted by James Reston in the *New York Times*, February 2, 1958.

political turmoil. We protect our judges from arbitrary political pressure by giving them long or life tenure, removable only by impeachment proceedings. But we expect from them a corresponding restraint in their political conduct. We expect them to forego partisanship, to refrain from making political speeches, to keep above political intrigue. Even in his private life we expect the judge to be a segregated man.

Among our military men the tradition has been to keep the military out of politics and politics out of the military. The Joint Chiefs of Staff attempt to advise the president and his civilian adviser from the purely military point of view. In a democratic society it is of the utmost importance that domestic politics and military considerations be kept in as distinct compartments as possible.

But consider the case of General MacArthur. Here we have a man of the highest competence in his particular field who had perhaps an even lower opinion of the political leadership under which he was carrying out his military responsibilities than that expressed by George Kennan. General MacArthur frowned upon any communication or contact between his subordinate officers and the executive branch of the government in Washington. He himself refused to go near Washington while Mr. Roosevelt or Mr. Truman remained in office. He carried to an extreme the thesis that the great specialist and expert is entitled, when serving his government, to a complete exemption from domestic political responsibility and even from contact with those who happen to be carrying the burden of executive leadership.

Many of the scientists would like to carve out a similar area where they can carry out what they consider to be in the national interest in the realm of science without political interference. George Kennan would exempt, as far as may be possible, the field of diplomacy from direct political interference and turn it over to the substantial control of the trained diplomatic experts.

At one time it was proposed by a very able group of physical and social scientists that a headquarters for the conduct of the cold war be set up in Washington. It would be unpublicized, manned by experts, and would issue instructions to the secretary of state, the secretary of defense, our economic agencies, the Voice of America, and even to the military. It would thus give expert coordination and direction to our struggle with the communists free from the handicap of political accountability. It seemed to me at the time that this was the ultimate *reductio ad absurdum* of the tendency of our experts to attempt to create walled off and exempted centers of specialized power and authority separated from political responsibility and accountability. It seemed to me a project to be fought with all the energies at one's command. What survived of this project was the Psychological Strategy Board which subsequently became the Operations Coordination Board. But both of these boards as finally established were firmly subordinated to politically accountable direction in the person of the undersecretary of state.

It is conceivable, had the right experts been chosen and given fuller powers than they were given, that they could have done a better job than has in fact been done. But who is to assure that the right and not the wrong experts are chosen? And are those who have to produce the necessary resources, to provide the military man power, and who have to bear the ultimate risks, to have no voice in the policies decided upon? In a democratic society how does one assure that there is consent for the policies adopted unless the responsible officials are politically accountable?

The Kennans, the MacArthurs, and the Oppenheimers may well be more competent in their chosen fields than are those who are politically accountable. The point is that one group of men is politically accountable—the other not.

Furthermore, a special effort is required for the expert to abandon concentration upon his chosen field and broaden his interests and temper his judgments to that humanity which is necessary to deal successfully with politics in a democracy.

Dr. Robert Elliott Fitch deals with one aspect of this as it bears upon the scientist: " . . . the scientist is prone to fall into three errors with reference to public affairs. He may, like the medieval anchorite, withdraw from society by living in the cell which is his laboratory. Or, emerging from his cell, with its austere discipline and chaste aspirations, he will be profoundly shocked to see the way his truth and power are prostituted to ends with which he cannot become reconciled. He will then do like all pietists before him: propose simple solutions to complex problems, see all issues naively and out of context, and make absolute moral judgments where the need is for shrewd compromise.

"The third possibility is that, being vain even as other men are vain, he will accept the inducements that are offered to him from every hand, will bestow an indiscriminate blessing upon whatever enterprise will ensure him the prestige and perquisite which he feels are his due.

"There are ways that do not lead to such dead ends for the scientist, but they are difficult ways. One is the way of a Conant or a Killian: deliberately to enter into the experiences and to assume the responsibilities and the disciplines that have to do with the art of human relations. The product of this dual discipline, in the scientist-statesman, can be one of our most valuable public servants in times like this.

"For those who do not have a genius for the double task, there is another choice. This is simply to put their truth and their power in the service of a democracy instead of in the service of a tyranny. In a free society the scientist will play his role as citizen like anyone else. The new priest like the old priest will have to learn that, no matter how potent the mana that he commands, no matter how great his power and his truth, he is not vested with any peculiar authority to decide on its uses. In a democracy, that authority resides in all persons alike."[4]

A question, however, can be asked about the last sentence of this quotation from Dr. Fitch's views. It is not clear that in a democracy effective authority resides in all persons alike.

The other day an astute observer commented on the viewpoint of Mr. Nehru. Someone had said that Mr. Nehru is sympathetic to American democracy. This observer suggested that a distinction should be made between Mr. Nehru's view of American political institutions, its economic system, and its cultural democracy. He suggested that Mr. Nehru approved our democratic political institutions, that he believed we just did not understand economic democracy which, in his opinion, required far more social orientation and governmental direction, but that he positively disapproved of what he understood to be our democratic

---

[4]"The Scientist as Priest and Savior," *The Christian Century*, LXXV (March 26, 1958), p. 370.

culture. As he understands American culture, it comes up
from below and amounts to a vulgarization of all values.
Mr. Nehru is obviously wrong about American culture. The
learned and the wise do have a special role in developing,
in preserving, and in propagating our cultural values. But
they do it not through the coercive power of the state.
They do it by the accountable process of persuasion and
consent.

Similarly our political leaders have a special share in
political authority. But theirs is an accountable authority,
not an arbitrary authority.

I have dealt at length with the role of the specialist,
the learned man separated from, or exempted from, political
authority and accountability. But learning and wisdom are
not the monopoly of those so exempted. The hope of the
democratic system depends upon the opposite proposition—the
proposition that men of general wisdom will in fact be
selected to carry political responsibility and accountability.

It undoubtedly has been true that in the great days of
American political development we have had men of learning
and of general wisdom in the politically important offices.
During the days of Washington, of Benjamin Franklin, of
Adams, of Jefferson, of Madison, I can hardly imagine that
the issue could have arisen as to the relation between the
man of political responsibility and the man of wisdom. They
obviously went hand in hand.

In the post Civil War era they quite clearly did not go
hand in hand. *The Education of Henry Adams* and Henry
Adams' *Democracy* give one an insight into the frustration
felt by a learned man, anxious to play a role in government
but unable to stomach the compromises that the politics of
the day made mandatory.

I am reminded of the testimony of Albert Speer, the
Nazi Minister of War Production, when we interrogated him
at the end of the war in Europe. Speer, who had been an
architect before the war, had demonstrated a phenomenal
versatility and power of mind in developing and maintaining
German war production despite the force of allied bombing
and the stupidities of Hitler's interference. I have rarely
met a more powerful intellect. We could not resist asking
him how it had come about that he had worked with Hitler's
gang and had let himself be associated with the inhumanities
and the stupidities of which they were guilty. He said it
was difficult for an outsider to put himself in the place of

a man torn by loyalty to his country and a political climate in which survival and power and the possibility of making some order out of chaos could only be achieved by associating oneself with people and with action of which one disapproved.

The other option, the option of opposition or of non-involvement, the option of Adenauer during the Nazi days, of Henry Adams, or of Plato, is more congenial but it also can have its frustrations and its tragedy.

It cannot be the good fortune of all mankind to live in Athens under the leadership of a Pericles, in Florence under the Medici, in the United States under a Washington or a Lincoln. Nor is it the usual fate of mankind to live under a Cleon, a Nero, a Stalin, or a Hitler and thus have an unambiguous case for withdrawal from government or opposition to it. The usual case is a mixed one in which the task of the learned man, the man of general wisdom and with a taste of politics, is to manage, to deal with, to nudge the existing situation toward the best that is within the realm of the politically possible, to find such scope as he can for his courage, his fortitude, and his willingness to view facts with an open mind. When given half a chance the combination of courage and an open mind can do wonders. This suggests a final quotation from Delcassé: "Take my word for it, *cher ami*, courage is the cleverest thing in the world."[5]

---

[5]*Three Critical Years: 1904-05-06*, p. 137.

"The Role of the Learned Man in Government" is reprinted with permission from *The Review of Politics*, 20 (July 1958), pp. 275-288.

3. Necessary and Sufficient Elements of a General Theory of International Relations*

(1959)

Discussions concerning a theory of international relations are apt to disclose what seems at first sight to be a paradox. On the one hand, they point to the need for a unifying conceptual framework comprising a manageably small number of conceptual elements and therefore for a high degree of abstraction. On the other hand, they point to the need to relax whatever system of concepts is used to

---

*The origins of the next essay may be traced to a paper, "The Implications of Theory for Practice in the Conduct of Foreign Affairs," that Nitze prepared in connection with his participation in an academic conference in Washington on international politics in May 1954, organized by Dean Rusk and Kenneth W. Thompson. As a result of that conference, he became part of an inter-university study group, which over the next several years held periodic seminars, sponsored by the Rockefeller Foundation, to discuss the theoretical aspects of international relations. In revising his earlier piece for publication with other papers generated by the study group's members, Nitze wanted to develop a conceptual framework that a practitioner, like himself, might find helpful in sorting out real-life problems. As Nitze explains, a viable and worthwhile theory is a complex thing—it must be sufficiently definitive so as to provide useful guidance, but it must also be open to adjustment in the light of continuing experience.

the complex worlds of general politics, of history, of philosophy and religion, and eventually to the infinitely complex living world of reality. On further consideration, however, these two drives—for abstraction and simplification and for wide relation—may not really be in conflict. In fact they may be mutually supporting.

In the field of the natural sciences it is hard to imagine a more highly abstract, succinct, and "elegant" equation than Einstein's famous equation relating matter to energy: $E = MC^2$. But this equation is meaningless unless viewed as a part of the immensely complex world of modern physics and mathematics. And many believe that to really understand why C^2, the square of the velocity of light, should appear in an equation relating mass to energy, one must go back to very deep philosophical and even metaphysical grounds.

Let us accept for the moment the hypothesis that one of the tasks of a general theory of international relations is the discovery of a relatively small number of abstract concepts which bear some continuing relationships one to another, an understanding of which relationships helps to illuminate and make more understandable the complex body of data comprised in the concrete world of international relations. There is a certain presumption in favor of a more elegant approach to this task, than of a more complex approach. In other words, on general grounds a three-element approach is preferable to a three-hundred-element approach. Simplicity has a virtue in itself, and one should not want to include any more elements in a theoretical structure than are necessary. But in addition to the criterion of simplicity and elegance there is the criterion of sufficiency. We must ask ourselves whether we have included sufficient elements for our theory to bear a meaningful relationship to the body of data it is meant to illuminate. In other words, the problem is one not just of demonstrating that this element or that element is necessary to a theory of international relations. The problem is rather one of finding what elements, in conjunction, constitute a necessary and sufficient foundation for a meaningful theory.

After this brief introduction it may be appropriate to summarize briefly the major theses of the body of this paper. The first thesis will be that a general theory of international relations needs to deal with the relationships between at least three fundamental concepts. These are structure, purpose, and situation. Power, and restraints on power, will be considered as subsidiary concepts within the system suggested by the three fundamental concepts. The second thesis will be that a general theory of international relations needs to permit of a multiplicity of viewpoints ranging from that of a responsible member of a particular group at a particular time (say, the secretary of state of the United States today) to one that approximates, as far as may be possible, to that of a hypothetical observer from Mars studying the emergent characteristics of an interacting system of many cultures, races, states, classes, etc., over the full course of history. The third thesis will be that a general theory of international relations needs to deal with two realms, the realm of fact and the realm of value—of "should" propositions—and with the interrelations between these realms.

In conclusion, the paper will touch upon the relation of the insights of a general theory of international relations to general politics, to history, philosophy, and religion on the one hand and to the living world of concrete action on the other.

I

We are all familiar with the proposal that "power" be considered *the* central concept of political theory. We are also familiar with the counter-argument that equally important with power, and conceptually prior to it, is the concept of purpose—the purposes to which power is directed. My suggestion is that even before one talks about purpose one has to be clear about whose purpose it is one is referring to and on whose behalf that purpose is directed—and that this requires an analysis of political structure.

I take it that individuals participate simultaneously in a wide variety of group structures. I have worked with Mr. Dulles and know something of him as a man and of his life as the senior member of an able and vigorous family. I know something of his relations with the law firm of Sullivan and Cromwell. I know something of his position in the Republican Party, of his role as secretary of state of the government of the United States, something of his role as the senior statesman of NATO, OAS, SEATO, etc., and something of his relationship to the Church and to the National Council of Churches.

The loyalties, purposes, objectives, principles and policies of each of these groups are far from identical. In part they converge, or reinforce each other, in part they are in conflict and create tensions and issues of divided loyalty.

Every participant in today's international scene, be he Gromyko, Nasser, a member of the Damascus mob, or a voter in the Polish elections, has similar complex group affiliations.

In developing a theory of international relations particular emphasis may properly be put on the particular group entity, the nation-state, which is presumed to have achieved a monopoly of the legitimate use of coercive force within the established geographic limits of its jurisdiction. There is a strong presumption that where such an effective monopoly exists there have developed strong ethnic, cultural, or other ties stemming from a shared historical experience.

Incidentally I take it that the word "international" in our topic is merely suggestive and is not meant to exclude, for instance, relations between the Greek or the Italian city states in another historical period just because the prime political units were then city states not nations.

The point is rather that even in a period in which the nation-state is predominant it cannot be considered absolute. It makes a substantial difference in international politics what the other and sometimes competing group structures are, what is the strength of loyalties and sympathies which they evoke, what is the content of the value structures which are associated with them.

The affiliation of each individual to the particular national group of which he is a member is not necessarily so overwhelming as to overcome all other loyalties, even as they affect international relations. In those instances where the purposes and interests of a nation are clear and unambiguous, national affiliation tends to overwhelm other sympathies. But the purposes and interests of nations are not always clear and unambiguous. Furthermore, the effective formulation of what a nation's purposes and interests are conceived to be, is much influenced by loyalties and sympathies which spring from participation in social groupings both broader than, and narrower than, the prime political entity.

In extreme cases it is hard to know whether the concept "nation" has any validity at all. Hungary may be a nation, and the common and intense experience through which the Hungarian people passed, during and after their ill-fated revolution, may weld them even more closely together as a nation. But the Hungarian government is hardly a national government. When one speaks of the purpose or the power of Hungary, what is it one is referring to? Obviously the struggle for power between the Kadar regime, backed by Soviet military force, and the mass of the population was far more significant than the power relationships between Hungary (conceived as comprising both its government and its people) and other national groups.

At this point I might comment that while I take seriously Whitehead's admonition against misplaced assumptions of concreteness I do not share the horror that many social scientists appear to have about the danger of reification in the use of abstract concepts.

There is not any doubt in my mind that the United States is a nation, in a very real sense, and that India has in recent years become one. Even though the word "nation" may be difficult to define it would seem to me that there is in fact a very real thing to which it can refer.

My point, therefore, is not that the nation is unreal; my point is that there are other things which are also very real—your family, my family, Sullivan and Cromwell, the State Department, Western civilization, the Christian religion—and that every individual participates in a variety of such very real entities.

It seems to me essential that any general theory of international relations have in it room for the consideration of the interrelated structure of these entities, not usually coterminous with national boundaries, which make competing claims on the loyalties, purposes, and actions of individuals.

In almost every problem of international politics the first question to be asked is, in the particular context, who is to be regarded as the "we" and who is to be regarded as the "they."

When Mr. Khrushchev and Mr. Gromyko address themselves to the Middle East, who in their minds is the primary "we" group, what are the other "we" groups in whose behalf they consider themselves to be acting, and what are the structural relationships between those "we" groups? Is it not likely that they put first the "we" group of the Communist Party Bolshevik, that the Soviet Union as a nation they consider to be "we" but in a secondary, not a primary sense, that the communist parties in Syria, Egypt, etc., they consider to be "we" but in a tertiary sense, in the sense of instruments to be used rather than prime participants in the group on whose behalf policy is being executed?

Similarly on our side, who do Mr. Eisenhower and Mr. Dulles consider to be the prime "we" group? Who are the other "we" groups whose interests they must take into account? Where does the NATO alliance fit into this structure? Where does Israel fit into it? Where do the Arab States, India, or the generality of mankind fit into it?

A case can be made that the first question, of politics in general and of international politics in particular, is whether, in what contexts and to what degree, people consider themselves to be part of a common "we" or opposed as hostile "theys." In other words political structure would seem to be one of the necessary primary concepts of political theory.

II

Let us assume for the moment that the question of structure has been taken care of and that, in the given context, we are clear as to the "we" and "they" groups we are talking about and their interrelations. Now what can be said about the concept "purpose?"

Perhaps a more useful phrase is the phrase "Value System." If we examine the attitudes of any organized group, let us take as an example the United States, we find a rich and diversified panoply of means and of ends and of general principles dealing with the proper relationship of means to ends. As we examine the ends in greater detail we find that they sort themselves out in a hierarchical structure. Certain of the ends, when looked at from above, appear to be means to higher ends. Certain of the means, when looked at from below, appear to be ends in relation to still more subordinate means. As we examine the principles governing the relating of means to ends we find that these principles fit in intermediate positions, higher than certain of the ends and perhaps lower than other ends.

The United States today undoubtedly considers a first-class air force capability to be a desirable end. In relation to that end, base agreements with Spain and Saudi Arabia, for instance, are desirable means. A first-class air force capability is in turn a means to the higher objective of an adequate posture of general military strength. A posture of general military strength is one of the means, among others, to general power in the international scene. Further up in the means-end chain is a still higher end. It is that an international climate be preserved in which political groups, organized in the manner of and for purposes similar to those characterizing the United States, can survive and prosper.

In such an analysis the difficult problems arise at two points. The most difficult problem is reached as one approaches the top of such a hierarchy. What are the central values which comprise the ultimate, non-contingent values of the group? One of these is probably survival of the group as a group. But related to this is the problem of the essential character of the group, to change which would be in essence tantamount to non-survival of the group.

The second difficulty arises in fitting into the hierarchy the general principles relating means to ends.

Effective opinion in the United States believes that force should not be used to settle international disputes, that binding contractual obligations of the United States government should be honored, that governments should generally be responsive to the will of the governed. If we were to consider settlement of a dispute vital to our survival, and believed in a given instance that it could only be resolved by force, I am sure we would resolve it through the use of force. There are a number of binding contractual obligations which the government has violated and where, under the actual circumstances which existed, I believed it was quite justified in doing so. We tolerate and even assist governments which are hardly responsive to the will of their people, and for very good reason.

The point is that the principles relating means to ends fit within the means-end hierarchy at varying levels and are not to be taken as absolutes standing outside that hierarchy.

The word "purpose" is often used in differing senses. Sometimes it is used to refer to the central values of a group, the loss of which would be tantamount to non-survival of the group. In this sense it refers to the top part of the means-principles-ends hierarchy. Sometimes the word "purpose" is used to imply the entire means-principles-ends hierarchy. It is used in this second sense in this article. When "purpose" is used to refer to the entire means-principles-ends hierarchy applicable to any given political group, or system of interlocking political groups, it seems appropriate to view it as another of the fundamental concepts in a general theory of politics and thus of international relations.

III

From the standpoint of a value system applicable to a particular nation, say the United States, "power" takes on the aspect of an intermediate means-end. Many of the subsidiary ends of United States foreign policy can be considered as means to the higher end of an increase in the general power of the country. But this increase in power is in turn a means to support the more general ends of that policy. The main point about power is that it is fungible, that it can be directed to achieving any one of a number of ends including particular ends which are not foreseen in advance. It is this aspect of power, its fungibility, which justifies the analogy which is sometimes drawn between the role of power in a theory of international politics and wealth in economic theory.

Because of its fungible character, an increase in power tends to become the end upon which statesmen and others dealing with foreign policy focus when the more general aims of foreign policy become confused or doubtful. It is possible, therefore, to construct a theory of international relations which assumes that power is in fact the ultimate aim of national foreign policies and to find that the analysis which flows from such a theory gives certain valuable insights into the real world of international politics.

Clausewitz in discussing military strategy starts off with an analysis of the "pure" theory of war. This "pure" theory assumes that no outside policy considerations will mitigate the natural tendency of war to degenerate to the utmost violence which the then state of military technology makes possible. But having analyzed this "pure" theory and drawn from it certain insights, he follows up by saying that no actual war has ever been fought according to the "pure" theory, that none ever will be so fought, and that it would be pointless and meaningless to do so. He then devotes much of his book to firmly subordinating military policy to the more general aims of political policy and thus more directly relates his theory to reality.

Even though analogies are dangerous, I would suggest that political theory in its treatment of power has a problem analogous to that faced by Clausewitz.

From the standpoint of the analysis of value systems associated with political groups, "power" is to be viewed not as a fundamental analytical category but as a subordinate element of the concept "purpose." For certain types of analyses in the field of international politics it may be fruitful to reduce the entire means-ends hierarchy to a competitive search for power. To do this involves a simplification comparable to the assumption that the nation-state is the only meaningful structural entity in the international scene and that the other complex structural elements may be ignored. Such radical simplifications are only useful if the analyst is quite conscious of what it is he is doing. Otherwise such simplifications may become over-simplifications.

IV

Let us now turn to the third fundamental concept suggested in the introduction to this paper, namely, the concept "situation."

Any analysis of politics requires reference to the facts of the situation in which the political events are assumed to take place. The set of facts which are relevant in a given instance may vary widely. They may be facts of geography, demography, the state of scientific knowledge, the stage of economic development, the availability of natural resources, the power of given weapon systems, etc.

A problem arises as to how the cut-off line is to be determined between those facts and values which are to be included within the concepts of "structure" and "purpose" and those to be included within the concept "situation."

The problem is analogous to that which one meets in mathematics in deciding which quantities are to be treated as variables and which quantities as parameters. It depends upon the field of interest of the observer. For the student of politics "structure" and "purpose" are at the center of his field of study and are generally to be treated as variables while climate, geography, or demography, for instance, are generally treated as parameters. These latter factors can change and in changing can modify the equations at issue but it is not these relationships which are usually the primary focus of interest of political theory. For the study of politics they can usually be assumed to have some reasonable but arbitrarily selected values so that the more interesting relations between the factors selected as variables can be explored.

V

At this point it may be helpful to say a few words about the second thesis mentioned in the introduction to this paper. This thesis is that a general theory of international relations needs to permit of a multiplicity of viewpoints, ranging from that of a responsible member of a particular group at a particular time to one that approximates, as far as may be possible, to that of a hypothetical observer from Mars studying the emergent characteristics of an interacting system of many cultures, races, states, classes, etc., over the full course of history.

If one attempts to get as close as possible to the viewpoint of the hypothetical man from Mars and looks at the classical period of the Greek city states, at the period of the Italian city states during the Renaissance, of the Warring States in early Chinese history, or of the European national state system during its heyday, certain common characteristics appear to emerge. It makes sense to talk of a common cultural base within which each system operated. Certain characteristic restraints on the unlimited exercise of state power developed. There was a consciousness on the part of the leading statesmen that they were part of a common culture and a common political system, that penalties could be expected if they adopted courses of action too violently inimical to the maintenance of the system and finally that there were certain types of action which they ought not to take. From this exalted view the system as a whole takes on the aspect of a group with an associated value system and sense of purpose. Mr. Toynbee advocates a focus on the history of civilizations rather than nations on somewhat similar grounds.

If one starts from the other end of the spectrum and views the problems of international relations from the standpoint of a given individual at a given moment of history, one gets a somewhat different slant, but there is still a certain degree of convergence in the final result. Let us take as our individual a member of the Policy Planning Staff of the Department of State as today's moment of history. I take this example because it is one with which I have been personally familiar.

This individual by his oath of office is required to uphold the Constitution of the United States and the faithful execution of the laws. His primary obligation is, therefore, to the United States as a nation-state, its value system and purposes, and its institutions. In developing his recommendations to the secretary of state, particularly on new issues—issues on which there is no body of tradition and no clear-cut guidelines have developed from previous national or congressional debate on the subject—he finds himself being led into the most searching and difficult avenues of value analysis. To what extent should policy be made on the basis of a "we" group extending out to include the peoples and governments allied to us? To what extent should the interests of the entire free world be considered? Are there issues on which the interests of mankind as a whole should be considered? Are there judgments as to equity and justice which flow not merely from the desirability that the United States as an organized group survive? Where are the grounds for a solid judgment on questions of equity and justice to be found: in natural law? in philosophy? in religion? What are the margins of freedom available to the United States within which it is possible both to promote the interests of the United States as an organized political group and also to promote more general standards of justice?

The point is that the framework of a general theory of international relations should be broad enough to encompass both points of view and points of view lying in between these extremes.

VI

As we have seen from the previous section, value propositions enter into our analysis even when we start from the most diverse points of view, that of the individual contemporary actor and that of the hypothetical man from Mars surveying the full range of history.

Value propositions can enter into the analysis, moreover, in two different ways. They can enter into the analysis from the standpoint of the actor, in which case they are of the nature of "should" propositions constituting the internal criteria bearing upon his decisions. They can also enter into the analysis as part of the "situation" with which the actor has to deal. Soviet doctrine, to the man in the State Department, is an assembly of "should" propositions which he must treat as objective facts not materially subject to change by anything he can do. They enter into his decisions as part of the "situation" in which the action he is contemplating must take place, not as internal criteria. The value system associated with his own position by virtue of his being an American, a responsible member of the United States State Department, and the kind of person he is, enters into his decisions in an entirely different way. Its "should" propositions have with respect to him an ethical, an imperative, quality.

Even the man approaching problems from approximately the position of the man from Mars is faced with the task of making a distinction between those "should" propositions he treats as matters of fact and those he uses as criteria by which he expresses approval or disapproval of what the various actors did or might have done.

Thus the third thesis of this paper, that a general theory of international relations needs to deal with two realms, the realm of fact and the realm of value—of "should" propositions—may need further expansion to include the two separate ways in which "should" propositions can enter into the analysis.

VII

It remains to consider the question of restraints on power.

These restraints may be of two kinds. They may be in the "situation." The factors of geography, the state of technology, the distribution of military power, etc., may be such as to preclude the free exercise of power beyond certain limits. The restraints may, however, be of entirely different nature. They spring from the system of values impinging upon a broad aggregate of states and other actors. They may impinge upon action directly through influencing the internal value system of the actor being considered. They may also be part of the external situation which he must consider in making his decisions.

Reinhold Niebuhr [dealt] with the relative position of the values "order," "justice," and "freedom" in the value systems, not just of individual nations, but across whole periods of history. He continues with an analysis of how changes in the position of these values came about in Europe and suggests reasons why the rising commercial classes needed a flexible instrument of political authority and why they needed the prestige of justice as well as the prestige of being the instrument of order to maintain the particular form of political authority which they had evolved.

I am told that President Eisenhower when he was deciding what action the United States should take after the British and French intervened in Suez wrestled with two questions. The first question was whether aggression is now obsolete as a means of settling disputes. The second question was whether it is possible to reserve the use of force to those cases where its use has a common sanction within the affected group.

It is not the purpose of this paper to go into the substantive issues involved in trying to find reasonably precise answers to these two questions. The point that I wish to make here is that the leading responsible statesman of one of the great powers today feels that questions of this kind are basic to the day-to-day decisions he must make. The United States is attempting to promote a tolerable degree of order in the vastly complex Middle

Eastern situation. The instruments of physical force which it has available for application in that area are extremely limited or else inappropriate as instruments to be applied to political problems of the nature of those there to be dealt with and managed. The other instruments of United States power which can be applied are also limited. It naturally becomes of the utmost importance to achieve a high degree of consent to such actions as we take, particularly if we must ever use military force. The degree of consent which we need cannot be achieved unless there is a reasonably wide acceptance in the area that our actions conform to and unless they tend to achieve some form of justice. A situation has developed in which there are, therefore, very great restraints upon the use of United States force, and perhaps to a lesser degree, upon the free exercise of other elements of United States power. . . .

A general theory of international relations which does not provide an adequate framework for the analysis of restraints upon the free exercise of national power would, therefore, appear to be insufficient and not closely enough related to the real world of international politics and the questions with which statesmen do in fact wrestle.

VIII

There is nothing particularly novel about the approach to a general theory of international relations put forward in this paper. Much of what seems to me to be the best work in the field does in fact fit within the suggested framework. What perhaps is distinctive is a matter of emphasis; a conscious effort on the one hand to grapple with concepts of a high order of abstraction and their interrelation, and on the other hand to relate these abstract notions to the broader fields of general politics, of history, philosophy, and religion. I believe that such a focus, if rigorously pursued, can open up new vistas of illumination. Without the use of abstract notions the field is far too complex to be grasped by the mind in any meaningful way. Without the relation to other fields the concepts become mushy and imprecise. The latter difficulty cannot be escaped merely by attempts at careful definition. The terms in which the definition is expressed generally lead back into broad areas of thought and of experience.

But let us suppose that we have made a certain degree of progress in our theoretical approach. How does one go about relating the insights obtained from theory to the world of practice? Here a process is involved which is the reverse of abstraction. Having cut off layer after layer of contingent detail in order to arrive at the essential core abstractions with which a theory can usefully deal, and having derived a certain insight from the manipulation of these abstract notions, we must then reverse the process and add layer after layer of contingent but relevant detail before we have something which may be applicable to the concrete world of human affairs. It is an accepted maxim that politics is an art and not a science. The final decision to take one course of action rather than another must be based on a human judgment involving a host of cross considerations. Judgments of this kind can only in part be based on rational intellectual processes. In large measure they must be a reflection of the character of the man, the nation, and the society that makes them. But there is still an element in the decision which is susceptible to human reasoning. And that reasoning can be better if it has available to it better theoretical and analytical tools than are available to it today. It is my belief that a general theory of international relations is possible and can supply such a tool.

From *Theoretical Aspects of International Relations.* Edited by William T. R. Fox. © 1959 by University of Notre Dame Press. Reprinted with permission.

4. A Framework of Theory Useful to the Practice of Politics*

(1981)

I. Introduction

    A.   Relation of theory to practice.

        i.   Simplification and abstractions or operational codes, implicit or explicit, are used by all, even the most non-theoretical practitioners.

        ii.   Simplifications and abstractions are necessary, but inadequate or dangerous if the theory is partial, internally inconsistent,

---

*Those familiar with Nitze's career and interests doubtless know of his founding role and close relationship with the Johns Hopkins University School of Advanced International Studies, or SAIS, which he helped to found near the end of World War II. From time to time since 1953, if he was not serving in government, Nitze has used SAIS as his base of operations. This involved, among other things, teaching a graduate seminar on foreign policy from an outline he first developed in the summer of 1954. Continuous revision over the years yielded the version included here, dated September 1981, the last time Nitze offered his seminar. As the outline indicates, Nitze employs a conceptual approach to policy, stressing the importance of ideas and cultural values in shaping a country's world view and role in world affairs.

or too narrow in scope to illuminate the specific problem at issue.

iii. Theory attempts to deal with the broad continuum of events, practice with particular nodes given importance by the immediately pertinent concrete situation.

iv. Theory can be useful but the limits of its applicability to specific situations need to be clearly indicated and understood.

v. Practice usually calls for some degree of new thought; cannot merely be deduced from past theory.

vi. Interaction between theory and practice improves both and makes them a developing art.

B. What is suggested is not necessarily new.

i. New theory is valuable only if it explains what was explained by prior art, and more besides.

ii. Prior art generally remains valid within certain specific limits.

iii. Changing context requires adaptation of theory and a new focus to maintain relevancy.

iv. Novelty in theory merely for novelty's sake can be dangerous.

C. Something is gained if the number of elements or concepts used in the theory can be kept to the minimum necessary to deal adequately with the subject.

i. This is analogous to the preference for the "elegant" solution in mathematics and physics.

      ii.   Oversimplification is dangerous in that it risks crucial variables being left out; in the extreme, this can lead to single value solutions which are almost always wrong.

      iii.   The attempt being made here is to find and set forth the necessary and sufficient elements of a theoretical framework useful to the study and practice of politics.

II. Individuals, Groups, and Political Institutions

A comprehensive theory of politics must deal, as one of its principal elements, with the relevant political structure. This structure varies with time, place, and the position and interest of the observer. It is the landscape within which politics take place.

A. Relations between and among individuals and groups.

      i.   Concepts of the nature and potentialities of man.

      ii.   The degree to which theory should emphasize the uniqueness of the individual versus the degree to which it should emphasize that actualizing his potential depends upon his roles in a social structure.

B. Overlapping social structure.

      i.   Individual, family, tribe, race, religion, state, nation, empire. An individual normally is part of many and possible all of these groups, a particular social structure and value system can generally be identified with each of them.

      ii.   There is a particular significance to the group claiming and exercising a monopoly over the legitimate use of force in a given area. Sovereignty is the word generally used to identify those making this claim; serious political problems, even revolution and war, are often associated with its breakdown.

iii.   In addition to formal groups, such as city, state, and nation, there are informal groupings that play an important role in any comprehensive theory of politics. They include elites, class, caste, party, functional groups, social groups, clubs. Related to this subject is the consideration of status and role of individuals in a given social and political context.

iv.   Supranational groups. The Catholic Church, the Communist Party (as distinct from the Soviet Communist Party), the Shiite, as opposed to the Sunni, Muslims.

vi.   Groups challenging ii. (And usually some elements of iii above).

C.   Political, social, and cultural institutions.

i.   Political - executive, legislative, judicial, constitutions, parties, elections, etc.

ii.   Political and social institutions - law, custom, tradition.

iii.   Social and economic institutions - public opinion, pressure groups, functional extra-governmental institutions (such as the Chamber of Commerce, the Atlantic Council, the CIO/AF of L, the World Council of Churches), etc.

III.   Value systems

A.   Each individual and group has a characteristic set of beliefs which guide his or the group's sense of what it should, or should not do, or approve of in the actions of others. These values tend to sort themselves into a hierarchical structure of values ordered in accordance with their relative positive or negative weight. Such a hierarchy of values associated with the full structure of interrelated social groups as they impinge upon each other, can be referred to as a "value system."

B. In examining a particular value system, it is useful to identify certain of its characteristics.

   i. For whom and against whom is the value system directed.

   ii. It is directed to promote the values of the "I", or of the "we" or to an understanding of the values of the "they."

   iii. In view of the fact that the individual is generally, if not always, a member of several interlocking groups, conflicts of loyalties between the interlocking groups of which the individual is a member constitute one of the basic issues of politics.

C. The Substantive Content of Value Systems.

   i. They may differ in their purpose, either in their manifest and declared purpose or in their latent and non-declared purpose.

   ii. In every value system one finds ends which are deemed desirable and approved actions consistent with those ends; they also contain ends and actions which are not considered desirable and means which should not or must not be used, even in pursuit of desirable ends. The latter include ethical constraints on the use of certain means. The hierarchy of ends in the value system thus becomes a hierarchal structure covering the use of appropriate means to obtaining the desired ends.

iii. Increasing the power of the "we" group versus the power, or potential power, of the "they" groups is in a somewhat different position than other ends in a value system. Looked at from the top of an ends/means hierarchy of values, power is a necessary means to achieve desirable values. Looked at from lower down in the hierarchy, increasing the relative power of the "we" group can appear to be an end in itself. Sorting out the ethical and pragmatic considerations involved in resolving these issues is one of the most difficult tasks both in working out a comprehensive theory of politics and in the practice of politics.

iv. As a help to resolving the issues outlined in iii above, political theorists have attempted to work out sets of principles as guides to and limitations on the choice of means. These can be useful but the task of making them comprehensive and widely applicable has thus far not been achieved.

v. Related to the issue touched on in iv above is the place to be given to "diversity" in a means/end hierarchy of values. In a U.S., or more generally, a free world theory of politics, it has a high position. In a totalitarian theory it would have no position or a minor position under the heading, "A Theory of Contradiction."

D. Intensity of the hold of value systems on individuals and groups.

i. Factors leading to, or indicative of, intensity are: scope of the value system, its internal consistency, its legitimacy, the breadth of the group's participation, its relevance to current problems, its challenge, its promises.

ii. Instance of insufficient or of excessive hold of value systems: Anomie is the sociologist's term for insufficient support from the society's value system for the mental health of its individuals. Excessive compulsion is the term describing the opposite situation. In extreme cases of either, statistics indicate an abnormal and sharp rise in suicide rates.

iii.   Pareto, the Italian sociologist, and others, have studied the distinction between what politicians say about the reasons for their actions (which Pareto called "derivatives") and the true reasons therefor which Pareto called "residues." Most cultures have developed other non-rational modes to express and to reinforce their value systems. The role and function of these non-rational elements of a culture merit a place in a theory of politics.

iv.   A distinction needs to be made between value systems which have grown naturally among the members of a political entity over the course of succeeding generations, and an ideology set forth by a great charismatic leader. The former is an organic growth, the latter is virtually complete as originally formulated.

E.   Criteria by which value issues should be judged.

i.   It is difficult to be impartial about one's own value system. But when one examines the value systems of other political entities and cultures as they developed, evolved, and sometimes ended, over the course of history, it may be possible to derive from that examination criteria to aid in judging the relative merit of specific value systems.

A common method is to compare them with values held by one's parents, grandparents and their ancestors; in other words by tradition. In an era of rapid change such as that of today, value problems are often quite different than those faced in times past and to which past value systems were relevant. One may start with the presumption that ancestral values had merit, but one should be willing to move forward when persuaded that traditional values are no longer applicable.

ii.   Some political theorists, such as Toynbee, suggest that the proper criterion to be used in evaluating a value system is the extent to which it can or has contributed to the survival of the political entities which adhere to it. But a review of the history of political entities, their value systems, and the length of their survival leads to serious doubt that this criterion can be considered absolute. Sparta had a unique political structure and value system which persisted relatively unchanged for some six hundred years. Athens continued unchanged for a lesser period. But it is not justified to place Sparta's value system on a higher plane than that of Athens. That of Athens provided far greater scope for creativity, beauty, and the full development of the potentialities of the human mind. Thus mere persistence does not appear to be an adequate criterion.

iii.   The student of a theory of politics is thus forced to the more basic sources of belief, to religion, to ideology or to criteria derived from philosophy, such as ethics, moral order, natural law, etc.

Because of the exclusivity of most religions and of all ideologies, they do not lend themselves easily to providing values for a comprehensive theory of politics providing general insights applicable across the world over broad periods of time in the past and hopefully for the future.

Perhaps the most hopeful approach is the careful and comprehensive study of history, winnowing out and eliminating those value systems that have encouraged repellent results and then attempting asymptotically to find systems of values which encouraged or produced more generally satisfactory results. From this could emerge the basis for a desirable value system for the future.

Having dealt with some of the structural aspects of social entities and their values, it is appropriate to turn to the issues relating to practice; i.e., how does one go about moving the objective political situation from where it is, closer to where one would like to see it be.

IV. **Fostering Favorable Change in the Objective Situation**

A. Estimates of the objective situation.

   i. The present objective situation and its past evolution.

   ii. Anticipated future changes in the objective situation and important variables, trends, and relationships governing such changes.

   iii. Knowledge, insight, simplification, standards of relevance, error, uncertainty, communication.

B. Estimates of the operational possibilities of effecting intended changes in the situation.

   i. Points at which the objective situation is subject to influence, guidance, or compulsion.

   ii. Alternative courses of action open for choice.

   iii. Limitations of change.

C.   Relating value systems to IVa and b.

    i.   Interests in the light of other value systems and the objective situation.

    ii.   Desires and objectives. Hierarchy in importance and in time phasing of objectives.

    iii.   Means as the aspects despite which one acts. Rationing of scarce means in amount and in time.

    iv.   Factors permitting cumulative or dynamic change in relative capabilities.

    v.   Intentions. Declaratory policy versus action policy.

    vi.   Interrelation of capabilities and intentions.

    vii.   Policy as generalized guides to action toward intended objectives.

D.   Relationship of process analyzed in IVc to decision-making and to action. Overlapping group values versus individual values.

V.   Principles and Techniques of Group Action

A.   Elements of group management.

    i.   Leadership - charismatic - collective-defused.

    ii.   Prestige - acceptance of the ends, respect for capacity to use means.

    iii.   Legitimacy - by historical precedent or traditionally approved procedure.

    iv.   Morale.

    v.   Myths, symbols, and ritual.

B. Issues of group management - the proper balance of:

   i. Power and responsibility.

   ii. Force and consent.

   iii. Politics from the barrel of a gun and complementary consideration of the values and cohesion of the "we" group.

   iv. Values applicable to the various "we" groups and those applicable to various "non-we" or "they" groups.

C. Modes of group action.

   i. Within a group.

     (a) Administration - hierarchical organization.

     (b) Role of committees, communication, education, planning.

     (c) Division and separation of powers - its advantages and problems.

   ii. Between groups.

     (a) Diplomacy.

     (b) Negotiation.

     (c) Conflict - grand strategy, strategy, and tactics.

   iii. Adjustments to reality and complementary considerations of increasing margins of freedom.

VI. **The Emergent Characteristics of Political Processes**

    A.   Rise and fall of cultures, city states, nation states, empires, civilizations.

    B.   Within sovereign entities.

        i.   Aristocracy to oligarchy to democracy to tyranny.

        ii.   Feudal to bourgeois to proletariat to dictatorship to some democratization.

        iii.   Processes of nonviolent change, growth, and decay.

        iv.   Processes of violent change - revolution and terrorism.

    C.   Within systems of sovereign entities.

        i.   Emergent characteristics of balance of power systems of alliances, coalitions, concerts, international, etc.

        ii.   Processes of nonviolent change.

        iii.   Processes of violent change - war.

    D.   Interrelationship between within-entity processes and inter-entity processes.

VII. **Methodological Considerations**

    A.   Abstraction versus the concrete.

        i.   Politics as an art.

        ii.   The role of individual personality.

        iii.   The role of accident.

B.   Asymptotic approach to truth versus relativity.

C.   Prediction, verifiability, sense of history.

D.   The concept of limits.

E.   The ideal versus the practical.

APPENDIX I

Applicability of Framework to Selected Historical Situations.

1. Thucydides and the Peloponnesian War.

2. Cleomenes III and the end of Sparta.

3. Li Chi Min and the founding of the Tang Dynasty.

4. Choshu and the Meiji Restoration.

5. Paleologue and *Three Critical Years.*

6. Cadogan's Memoirs, Moseley's *On Borrowed Time* and Munich.

7. *Arabia, The Gulf and the West*, J. B. Kelley.

8. *Facing Reality* - Cord Meyer on the CIA.

APPENDIX II

Applicability of Framework for American Foreign Policy for Major Current Issues.

1. International politics.

   a. Objectives, intentions, and policies vis-a-vis U.S.S.R.

   b. Regional Policy toward Europe, Gulf, Africa, etc.

   c. Arms control policy.

   d. U.S. coalition policy.

   e. Policies toward the third and fourth worlds.

   f. International economic policy, including natural resources.

2. Domestic politics.

   a. Sources of belief and values in the United States.

   b. Executive Branch relations with the public and the Legislative Branch.

   c. Overlapping loyalties and purposes in the U.S. - for a teacher, a businessman, a bureaucrat, a military officer, a politician.

5. The Recovery of Ethics*

(1960)

I. IDENTIFYING THE ISSUES

One large overarching problem and several smaller subsidiary problems emerge from most discussions of ethics and foreign policy. The big problem is the perennial one of the relation between our convictions about what is right, what is good, what ought to be, and our reading of what we can effectively do in the context of the real situation which confronts us in the world. Everyone faces up to this issue in some manner, but the balance is struck at different points and in different ways by different persons.

At one extreme are those who begin with a more or less absolute, clear and ideal conviction of what is right and good (what God wills or requires) and who insist that it is the church's and the Christian's primary duty to preach and to witness to that. To those who take this extreme position, calculations of what is feasible in the real world

---

*In this paper, Nitze made a bold and imaginative venture into the realm of moral philosophy and its implications for the content and conduct of American foreign policy. He develops his argument around the Thomistic assumption that there exists an irreducible ethical framework that can be approximately realized. In Nitze's view, it follows that the application of such a framework is of vital importance to clarifying the purpose, or intrinsic goals, of the country's foreign policy. Instead of handing down hard and fast answers, Nitze tries to suggest the broad criteria that must be considered in arriving at an ethically sound and viable foreign policy.

are largely irrelevant. The focus is on ideal ends rather than on effective means.

It is important to note, however, that the more "idealistic" positions do not ordinarily assume that the results of single-minded dedication to ideal ends imply any tragic choice between the ideal and the feasible. Rather they tend to read the realities in the light of the ideal, and to assume that a sufficiently imaginative effort to achieve those ideals will meet with success. They do not ordinarily say: Witness to these ideals, no matter what comes. Rather, they say: Follow these ideas, and the world will be made over. The insistence, for instance, that we need "massive efforts at negotiation and reconciliation, massive efforts at universal disarmament, massive renunciation of efforts contemplating war" surely implies that what is now lacking is sufficient dedication to the ends of reconciliation and peace, and that an analysis of the objective conditions influencing the attainment of these aims, and of the alternative courses of action which might in fact lead to a more tolerable and desirable situation, is of secondary importance.

On the other side of this issue are those who insist that the consequences in history of *political* action have to be assessed for the moral quality of that action to be known. They maintain that the intention alone does not decide the goodness or the badness of *political* acts. An important corollary of this more realistic conviction is that quite evil results may follow from quite good motives; that efforts to achieve ideal ends may not only fail but may produce evils quite contrary to their intent. This may come about by focusing on one goal where there are many to be considered and by wishful thinking about the possibility of achieving that one goal without sacrificing other and perhaps more important goals. Thus, one might answer those who recoil in moral horror before modern armaments by asking about United States responsibilities to preserve and carry forward the freedom of our own nation and that of other nations and our duties to the values and civilization we have inherited. Will we sacrifice all this as the price of our own moral fastidiousness?

Those who take a position in most extreme opposition to those who urge the primary importance of dedication to ideal aims are the group which seems to equate morality with the care with which decisions are made. It is their view that if the maximum possible care is taken to assess all the probable consequences of an act, before acting one thereby fulfills the requirements of morality. This group emphasizes the complexity of moral decisions in politics, the importance of careful consideration, the need to consider all the elements of the problem, and the checks and restraints of diverse views. In its most extreme form this view appears to deduce the aims of action from the probable consequences of the action and thereby becomes circular in its reasoning.

Obviously, the claim of ideal ends, and of principles ordering or restricting the means to be used in pursuit of those ends, are essential to any Christian political ethic. Furthermore, the Christian rejects any determinism of blind eminent historical forces and discovers both a measure of freedom for the will to affect history and a dimension beyond history in which acts have a meaning greater than their historical consequences.

How can one best summarize the conclusions that seem to flow from these extreme positions? On the one hand, I find unsatisfactory the position of those who would concentrate solely upon ends and principles ordering the use of means. On the other hand, I find equally unsatisfactory the position of those who would look solely to consequences. It appears to me that an adequate approach requires concurrent consideration of ends and principles, on the one hand, and of the consequences which are likely to flow from a given line of action in the concrete and specific situation in which the action is proposed, on the other hand. In other words, I do not reject the extreme "idealist" position and the extreme "realist" position in favor of some middle road. Rather, I think that a more elaborate analysis is needed—one involving *both* a consideration of aims and an assessment of probable consequences.

II. THE ROLE OF THE CHURCH

Let me turn now to a different aspect of the same problem. This has to do with the specific role of the church with respect to the problem of ethics and foreign policy.

A case can be made for the proposition that many other people will advocate the claims of practicality and

realism and that it is the role of the church to
counterbalance these claims by advocating the counter-claim
of ideal aims and principles. Thus a person who has arrived
at a resolution of the issue of "idealism" versus "realism"
similar to the one suggested above may still believe that it
is the particular function of the church to advocate one
part of the equation and to leave to others advocacy of the
other. He may say: There are many groups and persons
speaking up for realism, self-interest, and military
preparedness; there are also people, such as the president
and the secretary of state, whose special function it is to
sort out and judge the various claims that are put forward
and who are responsible for decisions governing a foreign
policy which takes into account the consequences of its
actions; the task of the church is not to do either of these
things, but is to urge the ideal claims which otherwise may
be overlooked. The church's role is that of the advocate,
not the judge. It is history finally that makes the
resolution of the many claims; it is the church's role to see
that the ideals she speaks for are not absent from the
resolution.

To this the reply may be made that though the
church's role as to issues of political policy is different
from that of a policy-making agency, it still must begin
with a realistic awareness of the possibilities of the world
before its witness to ideas—its advocacy—can be oriented as
to be likely to advance its own cause. When the church
gets into issues of foreign policy, it does not restrict itself
to the traditional precepts of Christian ethics, it begins to
apply its special background to a specific field of modern
existence. As it does so, some regard must be given to the
special characteristics of that field; its judgments about
reality must be hard-headed and must accord with the truth
insofar as it can be discovered; and at least a preliminary
attempt must be made to trace the probable consequences of
the positions advocated.

In summary of this point, even when one thinks about
the special role of the church, it is not possible wholly to
get away from the considerations discussed under the first
point: the need for an analysis which takes into account
both aims and the probable consequences of action.

My own background is not primarily church-oriented.
My particular orientation has been toward action and policy-
making in the business, military, and political fields. Those

of us with such an orientation are apt to put primary emphasis upon a realistic appraisal of the world as it is and a painstaking calculation of the probable results of alternative courses of action. Our first instinct is to leave to others the discussion of ultimate aims and principles. We tend to feel that common sense gives us a firm enough grasp on proximate aims and principles, and that our job is to get something done and have it work as we intend it to work. We recognize that those proximate aims and principles derive from and are geared into a deeper and more basic system. But we are apt to feel that our forefathers did a very good job of thinking through that more ultimate system and that there is not much use in our tinkering with it. We will give it our full respect, and will be guided by the related precepts for action which have been handed down to us by tradition. Our main job is to act and to act wisely and successfully within that framework.

But then, situations arise in which the proximate aims and principles derived from the system handed down by tradition do not seem to be adequate. They seem to lead to inconsistencies and, in extreme cases, to antinomies when applied to the newly emerging and basic problems turned up by the dynamic and threatening world in which we live today.

In such a world, even the man primarily oriented toward action finds himself forced toward a re-examination of the ends and principles underlying his proximate aims. He turns to the church for guidance. And at that point he may find the church not much better equipped than he to supply the answers that he needs. Both are groping. They start from different initial positions. Neither sees clearly where clarification can be found. It is possible they can help each other. Both churchmen and men of action in the political field can profit from the interaction of each other's ideas. The academician also has something to contribute to the process.

III. THE PROBLEM OF VALUES

Several points which have arisen in recurrent discussions with my students have a bearing on the issue of ethics and foreign policy and merit mention at this point.

At one time much of the new and more advanced analysis of political theory coming out of the academic world in the United States seemed to be based on the thesis that aims and principles—what the behavioristic and positivistic authors referred to as "value preferences"—were somebody else's business and that the political scientist should restrict himself to considering the facts of the real world and the types of action which could be expected to produce given results.

Subsequently a number of writers on the subject of political theory developed a somewhat different approach. In this approach values, in other words, aims and principles associated with a given group or political system, are determined by the needs, or in technical language, the functional requirements, of the group or system.

This approach has the virtue of reintroducing values, and thus aims and principles, into the field of political theory. To my mind, however, it suffers from certain defects. In the first place, it tends to underplay the complex interrelations between, on the one hand, individual persons and the values immediately associable with persons and personality, and, on the other hand, the complex structure of groups in which individual persons may participate: the family, the corporation or labor union, the political party, the nation, the church, and the culture or civilization of which they are a part.

There obviously are values, values of survival, of development, of the full actualization of potentialities, associable with the individual person and with each of the groups or systems in which he may participate. To the student of politics the nature of these values, their origin, modification, and relation to the functional requirements of the individual or of the group of which the individual is a member, and with which values are associated, is of interest in throwing light on the nature of the real world which he is trying to understand.

There is, however, more to the problem of values than this. In the first place, conflicts of value arise between personal values and various group values, and between one set of group values and another set of group values. It is often emphasized that the ideal situation is one in which there is convergence and mutual support between these interlocking value systems. The individual may find the opportunity for the realization of his highest potentialities, for instance, within a loving family and as part of a productive business organization operating in a progressive state—the state playing a responsible role in a just international order of some kind.

But convergence and mutual support of the value systems of interlocking and interacting groups do not always take place. Potential conflict is always present. It seems to me that the principal task of ethics and morality is right here; its task is to give some guidelines to the resolution of potential conflict between the various parts of a very complex individual-group structure and of the value systems associated with those parts. Perhaps it would be useful to make a distinction between the concept "value" and the concept "ethical framework." The distinction would be that "values" apply to an individual or to a specific group; "ethical framework" would apply to the broader standards by which conflicts between such values may be resolved.

IV. INTERRELATED VALUES

One method of resolving potential conflict is to subordinate or to order the relations between the individual and the various groups, or of one group to another, in a manner depending upon the context in which the issue arises. Thus the individual is expected to subordinate certain of his values to those of the system in which other individuals, as well as he, can survive and have an opportunity to actualize their potentialities. If the context is such that the system as a whole is threatened, he is expected, if necessary, to lay down his life for it. In the political system which has arisen in the modern era, the nation-state is presumed to have a monopoly upon the legitimate use of coercive force. In contexts where the issue of the possible use of coercive force arises, the individual and all sub-groups within the territory of the nation-state are expected to subordinate their actions to those of officials acting on behalf of the nation-state. But in states democratically organized the use of coercive power by the state or its agents is hedged in by a number of restraints. In our country it is hedged by a Constitution, a separation between the executive, the legislative, and judicial branches, by the right of *habeas corpus*, jury trial, and due process.

Thus in the domestic political scene we have not just a partial subordination of the individual and sub-groups, such as the corporation, labor union, or political party to the state, but an ordering of the relations between them.

I find that it is hard for many of my students to grasp the interrelations between the various elements of a political system. They tend to advocacy of polar positions. They feel that they must choose between dedication to the individual and values associated with the individual, or dedication to the nation and the values associated with the nation. They feel that they must choose between being for the use of force in behalf of the preservation of the integrity of the state, or being against the use of force and for the principle of government solely by consent.

They do not easily understand that the individual person and the political order in which he lives are interconnected as are space and time; that it is hardly possible to speak of one without implying the other.

If the considerations I have been advancing with respect to the arena of political relations within a state have validity, several consequences would seem to flow therefrom for the application of ethics to politics within a state. In the first place, it would seem unjustified to associate morality with the values of any single portion of that political world. It would be wrong to associate the ethical position solely with the values of the individual, the values of the family, the values of the business or the labor world, or the values of the state alone. Neither would it seem justifiable to associate the concept of ethics with an absolute dedication to the use or non-use of a particular type of means, for instance, the non-use of coercion. Morality would seem more appropriately to be associated with a point of view which stands above these immediate political issues and which finds guidelines either in tradition or in the deeper truths revealed by nature and by religion that tend to give point, order, and harmony to the resolution of those issues.

V. INTERNATIONAL OBJECTIVES

International politics presents even more difficulties, as a field in which to sort out the role of ethics, than does the field of domestic politics.

In the international arena, no one has a monopoly of the legitimate use of force and the most basic values may be in conflict—even the values associated with the survival of entire nations or civilizations.   There is no executive controlled by a constitution, balanced by a judicial and a legislative branch and subject to the restraints of *habeas corpus* and due process.   But even the international arena need not be wholly without order.

From 1815 to 1914, a certain degree of international order was maintained.   The balance of power system among the European states preserved a certain degree of stability. England, with control of the seas, could act as a balance wheel.   Economic institutions based on the gold standard and centering on the London capital market provided an economic framework within which large portions of the world, including the United States, were able to make tremendous forward strides in developing their economies. Above all, wars were kept limited as to objective and limited in extent.

The two world wars shattered the system which existed prior to 1914.   Today the fundamental issue in the international arena is that of who will construct a new international order, appropriate to today's world, to take the place of the one that was shattered in those two world wars.

Until the spring of 1947, we in the United States did not face up to the fact that that was the issue and that we had to do something about it, because no one else had the will or resources to do it.   Few of us remember the intense activity of the six months beginning in March 1947 with the Truman Doctrine, announcing our determination to help those willing to fight for their independence.   This was followed by the Greek-Turkish Aid Program, the merger of the Western zones of Western Germany leading to restoration of German sovereignty, the Marshall Plan, the Rio Treaty, and the National Security Act of 1947, creating the Defense Department, the Central Intelligence Agency, the National Security Council, and the National Security Resources Board.   That intense activity in 1947 was subsequently followed up with the filling out of our treaty arrangements, including NATO and the ANZUS Pact, the Mutual Defense Assistance Act, Point Four, the restoration of sovereignty to Japan and, finally, the decision to intervene in support of the Republic of Korea against overt aggression.

As one looks back on the overall pattern of the actions undertaken in those years, one can ask what is it we were trying to do? I think one can summarize it by saying that we were trying to lay the foundations for an international system which would substitute, in the circumstances existing in the modern world, for the system which the balance of power in Europe, supported and managed by the British—relying on their control of the seas—had maintained during the century following the Congress of Vienna. This new structure had to have its political, its economic, and its military aspects. It had to provide for certain overall world-wide functions within which closer regional institutions could be developed. A unique role in this system had continuously to be borne by the United States because we alone had the resources and the will to tackle the job. And while this system was being developed it had to be continuously protected against the hostile and destructive efforts of the Soviet-Chinese Communist bloc which was dedicated to the construction of another and antithetical system.

Let us take a look at the main elements of the structure we were trying to erect and to defend while we were erecting it. One important part of the structure was its economic part. This had its worldwide aspects geared into the United Nations structure. The International Monetary Fund provided an institution looking toward greater stability of the currencies necessary for the financing of the world's commerce. The International Bank for Reconstruction and Development was to provide a pool of capital to flow to those areas needing capital and able to make sound use of it. The General Agreement on Trade and Tariffs was to move toward the reduction of administrative barriers to international trade. These international instruments were reinforced by regional and bilateral actions such as the Marshall Plan, the Organization for European Economic Cooperation, the European Payments Union, the Technical Assistance Program, and the Colombo Plan. And these international, regional, and bilateral approaches were supported by United States economic policies generally consistent with our new role as the world's leading creditor nation and principal reservoir of capital and of technology.

In the military sphere a similar structure compounded of international, regional, and individual arrangements was gotten under way. The heart of these military arrangements had to be strength at the center, strength in the United States itself. The need was early foreseen to give this strength at the center greater flexibility than was provided merely by SAC and its nuclear armaments. It was only as a result of the attack into Korea that appropriations could be secured for anything approaching an adequate effort in that direction. Supplementing United States strength at the center, a major effort was gotten under way to build strength at the periphery through NATO, through the MDAP program and through our bilateral arrangements with the ROK, the Chinese Nationalists, and Japan. Finally a German contribution to European defense was sought but ran into very great difficulties. An attempt was made to spread this system to the Middle East through the project for a Middle East Defense Organization—but that effort foundered because of Arab disunity and the strains caused by the Arab-Israeli controversy.

The economic and military measures found their place within a political structure whose broadest aspect was the United Nations Organizations and whose heart and driving spirit were United States responsibility. There emerged a pattern of political relationships characterized by exceptionally close collaboration among the United States, England, and Canada, spreading out through close, but not as close, relationships with Germany, France, Italy, and Japan, and shading off to cooperation on certain basic matters with the uncommitted but free countries such as India and Burma.

The object was to create a structure sufficiently flexible to house the diverse interests and requirements of the entire non-Communist world. Even with respect to the Communist world it was hoped that the structure would have something to offer and would, by its attractive power, either draw off portions of the Communist world, as it did in the case of Yugoslavia, or result in a weakening of the bonds within the Communist world, as it did in the case of Poland but failed to do in the case of Communist China.

In 1952 and 1953 only a portion of the United States population was persuaded that an effort as enormous as that entailed in the construction and maintenance, with the United States bearing the principal responsibility, of a new international system was really necessary. Could we not look more to our own interests as a nation and leave to others the worries about an international system? Others thought that so burdensome an external policy would inevitably prove inconsistent with the preservation of our domestic political traditions. Still others thought that, though the aims of our foreign policy might be all right, there must be some easier and cheaper way of going about the business. And there were those who were disappointed in the prospect of an effort extending indefinitely into the future. If we not only had to get such a system going, but then had to keep it going, in spite of the apathy of a large portion of the world and the bitter hostility of another large portion, would we not be at the job forever?

Changes reflecting this national mood were made in the program in an effort to meet the popular objections to the previous program. One result was that public opinion within the United States was consolidated, at least the most serious schizophrenic strains in the body politic were suppressed. But in my view, the program as a whole suffered and our national strategy became less clear in direction and less effective in execution.

To my mind, the most serious modification in our national strategy in the period beginning in 1953 was the decision to emphasize that our first aim was to pursue United States national interests and to play down our interest in the construction of a working international order. The moment we began to emphasize that our policy was directed primarily to the pursuit of United States aims and interests, other nations were forced to look more closely to their own narrow interests. If we were to focus on United States interests, rather than on the creation and defense of a system under which we, along with other independent nations, could survive and prosper, the British were bound to look primarily to United Kingdom interests and the French to French interests.

If the nation, or nations, principally responsible for a given international system appear to lose faith in that system and appear to be following their narrow national interests, the other nations of lesser power are bound to become uncertain in their policy. These lesser powers know they, without the cooperation and leadership of the greater powers, cannot hope to make the system work. They must then decide whether the faltering by the great powers is temporary or whether they must prepare to adjust themselves to some quite different system.

In my judgment, the course of events which ended up in the Suez crisis was in part attributable to this change in our national strategy. It can be argued that the change was largely one of emphasis in presentation and not one of substance. Changes in presentation are likely, however, to result in changes of substance even if not originally intended.

The other modification which seemed to me to be serious was the effort to cater simultaneously to those who wanted a quicker solution and those who wanted a less burdensome effort. We thereby encouraged anticipations and actions which we were in no position to back up. It can be argued that our emphasis upon a policy of liberation had little effect in stimulating the Hungarian uprising. In my view it did have some effect. But it can hardly be argued that we were in a good position to back it up when it did occur.

By the summer of 1957 we had experimented with a series of modifications to that national strategy which had evolved during the period 1947-1952. The modifications, however, had not met with success and we had been forced back by the hard facts of the situation to more or less the same general policy line from which we had started. During that summer the studies of the Gaither Committee and of the Rockefeller Committee reaffirmed that there was no easy or cheap short cut to national survival in today's world; that we needed flexible military strength at the center, that we needed allies in depth and at the periphery, and that, above all, we needed a functioning world political and economic system in which the United States must play a continuing and leading role.

With Sputnik we entered into a new and even more disturbing phase. It is easy to over-emphasize the Sputniks. We had known earlier that the Russians were probably ahead of us in the ballistic missile race. We had known from the very beginning that we must count on some time eventually arriving when our technological lead in atomic weapons would be less important, or perhaps of no importance. We knew about Russian economic advances and the percentage of their gross national income which they were putting into defense and the expansion of their industrial base.

The convergence of three separate sets of factors gave a new look to the situation in the fall of 1957.

One of these factors was Sputnik, and the confirmation which it gave to what we had known, but had not really believed, about Russian economic, technological, and specifically missile progress in recent years.

The second was the rapid political recovery which the Communist central authority seemed to have made from the strains which had been increasingly evident during the period prior to the Polish and Hungarian crises. Khrushchev, after the suppression of the Hungarian revolt, had apparently solidified his position within the top leadership; the top leadership had strengthened its position within the Party and the state; and the Russian Communist party had reestablished its authority over all the satellites other than Yugoslavia. One faced the prospects of a long pull before any serious internal political weakening of the opposing forces could be expected.

And, thirdly, the internal political situation in France, India, Indonesia, the Middle East and Africa looked far from healthy.

In such a situation the Russians could be expected to work out some gambit which, in their estimation, was well designed to encourage the divisive factors in the West and to give themselves a good platform from which to pursue their efforts to nail down an international system compatible with their aims rather than ours. The gambit of proposing a summit meeting about Berlin and Germany was admirably designed to do just that.

The resulting debate, which has gone on more intensely in Europe than in the United States, has not been about whether or how we in the West should design an international system which will be attractive to and have a place in it even for countries not behind the Iron Curtain. Under the appearance of debating disengagement in its various forms, including unilateral nuclear disarmament, the debate has been about the question of whether, within the international system proposed by the Soviet Union, there may be a place within which presently independent countries can survive without complete loss of that independence. The alternatives which have been debated have been on the one hand the prospect of nuclear war, on the other hand the prospect of an international order compatible with the aims of the Soviet Union and international Communism but offering, within that framework, coexistence to the West.

The point of this analysis is that the principal issue before the world is what kind of international order will prevail in the future. Will it be one compatible with ideas, principles, and political structures such as those we enjoy in the United States while offering a place within that structure to Communist states? Or will it be an international structure designed by and compatible with the objectives of the Communist states while offering a possibility of coexistence to us and to other states similarly organized? I frankly doubt the possibility of a truly halfway position. I can imagine a system compatible with our ideas under which the U.S.S.R. would have rights and responsibilities as great as those of any other single state. Similarly within an international order basically designed by the Communists I can imagine them granting more or less freedom to the United States and other countries similarly situated. But the essence of the two systems would be quite different. If there is no middle ground, if this really is the issue, if this is what we mean by the struggle for peace with justice, what resources of will and of national sacrifice are we entitled, or obligated, to put into the effort to cause a system compatible with our values to prevail? What risks are we entitled to take with the awful hazard of a nuclear war? Do moral considerations give us any guidelines?

In recent years I have heard the most divergent viewpoints on this issue expressed with clarity and force. One viewpoint is that, in spite of the frictions, inadequacies, and inequities of our system, it is basically humane, progressive, dedicated to truth and to justice, and has a degree of validity such that any dedication of will and sacrifice of material benefit necessary to the creation of an international system compatible with its survival is a duty, an obligation, and a privilege which we cannot shirk.

The other view is that any confrontation of will between the Soviet rulers and ourselves over an issue so basic as that of the fundamental nature of the international order which is to prevail in the world, is likely to result in a nuclear war and that the upshot of such a war will be no system rather than their system or ours; and that therefore we should, if necessary, accommodate ourselves to their system preserving for ourselves and others as much freedom as they may permit.

These two positions do not quite meet in direct opposition because those upholding the first view maintain that, if our effort is intense enough, we can prevail in the establishment of a compatible system without having the situation degenerate into a general war. Nevertheless a reasonably precise issue is drawn.

To find grounds on which one can base a firm conviction one way or the other merits the most dedicated application of such capacities as are granted us.

VI. THE IMPLICATIONS OF SCIENCE

In the foregoing section I pointed up only one, in my view the most crucial but still only one, of the multitude of issues posing an ethical problem in the field of foreign policy. Obviously there are hosts of other such problems. Under what types of circumstances, if any, should we continue nuclear tests? Under what circumstances, if any, should we use non-nuclear weapons to enforce our views of what is just and equitable in the relations between nations? Under what circumstances, if any, should we use firm measures to keep our allies from engaging in unjust or imprudent actions? What non-coercive measures are appropriate to what kinds of international purposes? What economic or political sacrifices are we justified in making or requiring of others for what purposes? How should one choose between competing or conflicting political objectives or political groups?

It can perhaps be objected that these questions are too general to permit specific answers. But we still are faced with issues which involve ethical judgments even if we make our questions more specific. The more specific we make our questions the more significant become issues of fact. But even after we have settled all the issues of fact there will remain an irreducible element which poses an ethical judgment.

Others may object that many political questions can be resolved only by the competitive exercise of power and that ethical choice has little place. This objection also falls upon closer analysis.

Werner Heisenberg, the German Nobel physicist who developed the principles of quantum theory, tells a story which illustrates the point. He describes a conversation which he had with a theological student during the revolutionary struggles which racked Germany in 1919. Heisenberg was seventeen years old and was attached to a military unit in Munich during a period when the center of the city was occupied by Communists. Every noon the unit fetched its lunch from a field kitchen in the yard of a theological seminary. Heisenberg describes the discussion with the student as follows:

"One day we became involved in a discussion with a theology student on the question of whether this struggle in Munich was in truth meaningful. One of our group took the stand that questions of power could not be decided by intellectual means, by speech-making and writing; the real decision between us and the others could only be determined by force, he declared.

"Thereupon the theology student replied that the very question of who were 'we' and who 'the others' were obviously depended upon a purely intellectual decision, and that probably a good deal would be gained if this decision were made somewhat more intelligently than was usually the case. We could find no good reply to this argument." Heisenberg ends the story with the comment that perhaps it might not be so bad if we were to teach youth not to despise the values of the mind.

If it is true, as I believe it is, that foreign policy decisions along with political decisions in general involve an irreducible ethical content, how do we go about discovering the relevant ethical framework and how do we describe and justify the framework in terms which commend themselves to belief by the mind of the modern world? Many would say that these are the problems on which theologians and philosophers have broken their skulls for generations, leaving us in the state of intellectual chaos in which we now find ourselves, and that there is little hope that we can do better than to add to the confusion. I take a different view. It seems to me that there is today a convergence of a number of factors which give grounds for hope that rigorous effort can, in the not too distant future, restore a glimmering of light in the existing darkness.

One of these factors is to be found in the developments of modern science and in the implications for philosophy of those developments. One cannot read the more general writings of the leading contemporary scientists without coming away with the conviction that most of the intellectual blocks which classical physics seemed to throw in the path of belief in a meaningful ethic are on the way out. That blind mechanical determinism which flowed from Newtonian mechanics and which seemed inconsistent with ethically oriented and responsible human will no longer finds scientific support. Potentiality is restored to a position of reality. The gulf between mind and matter is no longer in principle unbridgeable. Man need no longer feel that there is an inherent contradiction between his instinctive knowledge that he is a part of a meaningful universe and a cold science, in which he felt he must believe because of its vast success in elucidating so much of the natural world, but which appeared to cut his essential spirit entirely out from that world.

One of the most important features of the development and analysis of modern physics is that, as knowledge expands, the concepts of ordinary language seem more stable than do precise terms of scientific language. The scientific language is derived as an idealization from limited groups of experimental phenomena. Scientific concepts are derived from experience by refined experimental tools and are precisely defined through axioms and definitions. Only through these precise definitions is it possible to connect them with a refined mathematical scheme and derive mathematically the full variety of phenomena possible in the particular field covered by the experiments. Scientific concepts provide a very close fit to the observable results of experiments upon that part of nature accessible to precise measurement and subsumable under mathematically tight deductive systems of scientific concepts. But they may not fit at all with other parts of nature. The concepts of ordinary, natural language, on the other hand, are formed by an immediate connection with reality over many generations. They represent reality over the full span accessible to the human mind, not merely that portion accessible to certain types of precise measurement. Ordinary language concepts may not be precisely defined but they do not lose touch with reality. They may be somewhat modified over the ages. But they are not subject to sudden and complete falsification by a few unexpected results of scientific experiment.

The general trend of thought in the nineteenth century had been toward an ever increasing and widespread confidence in the scientific method and toward a corresponding skepticism with regard to those concepts of the natural language, like mind, soul, life, purpose, duty, justice, and God, which do not fit into the closed frame of scientific thought. Twentieth century physics at first increased this skepticism, but then skepticism turned against the over-estimation of precise scientific concepts and finally against skepticism itself. It was finally realized that that part of reality covered by scientific concepts is very limited, and the part not covered by them is unlimited. "Understanding," even of the part covered by scientific concepts must always be based finally upon the natural language. Hence Heisenberg and others conclude that we must be skeptical about skepticism with regard to this natural language and the essential concepts referred to by it. In this way the door is reopened which seemed to be shutting on the possibility of an ethical view of the world not in contradiction with the modern world of science.

Similarly, the climate of belief with respect to all fundamental ideas of philosophy, the concepts of ontology, epistemology, of logic had shifted from that which pervaded much of the nineteenth century and much of this century. No longer do people look at one askance if one says that logical positivism is an inadequate approach to the sum total of reality. Today the writings of a man such as Charles S. Peirce, which received little public attention during his lifetime, are republished and widely commented upon. As confidence in the completeness of our understanding of the material structure of the universe has declined, the stature of the concepts of relation and of mediation has risen to a point where the reality of general ideas, such as duty and justice, is on a par with the reality of the concepts of atomic particles and of simultaneity and of position. And our confidence in our ability to know about and to reason with respect to these general ideas has similarly been restored.

The second factor which seems to me to converge in indicating that one can have grounds for hope that progress can be made in discovering an ethical framework commending itself to belief by the mind of the modern world is the factor of need. I do not mean to imply that merely because something is needed, it is possible. Rather my point is that when the need is not evident and immediate people are apt not to take the pains to get to the bottom of difficult questions. For many generations it appeared to Americans that this country was getting along very well indeed. Our founding fathers had wrestled with the basic question of the relationship of politics to fundamental philosophic and ethical concepts and had produced the United States Constitution. The political institutions which flowed from the Constitution might need minor modification from time to time, but there was little need to rethink the basic philosophic ideas behind them. That had been done and the results were obviously good. Any one who might try to tackle the extremely difficult job of thinking the problems through afresh must be some manner of crank. Today the context has changed. The future no longer looks obviously good. To tackle the job of thinking through to fundamentals does not today convict one of being a crank.

The third factor which impresses me is that ideas and ways of approaching the problem of politics and ethics are now being exchanged among those thinking and writing in this field which offer the prospect of clarifying and simplifying the analysis. These ideas may not be new. Most useful ideas are not novel. But in combination they suggest, to me at least, the possibility that a major step forward can now be made toward clarity and understanding.

VII. "WE" AND "THEY"

Let me mention a few of these ideas. First there is the idea that one of the basic questions of politics is that of the "we" and the "they." In any particular context, who is it that is considered to be "we" and who is considered to be the "they"?

Second, there is the idea that any individual participates in an overlapping system of a number of such "we" structures. Third is the idea that associated with each individual and with each group with which he is affiliated there are over-lapping systems of value which are connected with his purposes and the purposes and the functional requirements of each group.

Fourth is the idea that over and beyond the values of any particular array of groupings of human beings there exists an ethical framework which has objective validity, of

which men can aspire to have some degree of understanding—not perfect, but approximate—and which can give a
measure of insight and guidance to those who seek it.

An important thing about these four ideas in
combination is that they make possible a distinction between
the values associated with the purposes and interests of an
individual and the groups with which he is associated and
the ethical framework pursuant to which ethical judgments
as between conflicting value systems are to be judged. The
fourth idea, the idea that it is possible to rise above both
individual value systems and socially formed value systems
and obtain some approximate insight as to the nature of an
objective ethical framework over and above those value
systems is obviously closely related to the traditional
concept of natural law.

Let us briefly examine the problems of ethics and
foreign policy in the light of these four ideas. To be
specific let us assume we are looking at the problem from
the point of view of the secretary of state of the United
States.

The secretary has certain individual distinctions of
personal character and personal ambition. He has duties and
obligations to the State Department organization which he
heads and which looks to him for leadership. He is a
member of the executive branch of government, at present
operating under a mandate to the Republican Party and a
Republican President. He takes his oath of office to uphold
the United States Constitution and the faithful execution of
the laws.

Even in this highly simplified description of the
secretary's relationship to "we" groups internal to the state,
we see a complex of interrelated interests, duties, and
responsibilities—in short, values. Conflicts of values
associated with these different groups arise daily and must
be brought into convergence or resolved on some basis. In
this context, the primacy of values associated with the
nation can be presumed generally to take precedence over
those associated with the secretary as an individual, with
the State Department as an organization, or with the
Republican-controlled executive as a branch of government.
Nevertheless, even at this level, the harmonizing,
integration, and concurrent pursuit of multiple values are
involved.

When we proceed to the next level and consider the interplay of value systems on the international scene—from the standpoint of the American secretary of state—we run into similar complexities. The secretary has a primary obligation and responsibility to the interests of the United States as a nation-state; at this level the people of the United States are the "we", and all other peoples are the "they." The secretary, in representing the coalition system and alliance systems of which the United States is a leading member, has obligations and responsibilities to a much wider "we" group of nations and peoples. If the thesis advanced in Section V of this paper is accepted, the thesis that a principal task of United States foreign policy is today the construction and defense of a world system of order to replace that shattered in the two world wars, then the values to be pursued by the secretary of state include those associated with a "we" group virtually coterminous with mankind as a whole.

We have now reached a level of complexity which does not lend itself to simple methods of analysis. Not only are the value systems associated with each "we" group complex; we now have overlapping "we" groups of expanding comprehensiveness to deal with.

At this point a few general observations on value systems appertaining to an individual nation-state may be pertinent. No single value—such as survival, security, power, wealth, prestige, respect, influence, or freedom to actualize its potentialities without unwanted outside interference, can be posited as the supreme value in relationship to which the other values are to be regarded merely as means. Neither are principles ordering the relationship of means to ends to be regarded as absolutes. What is involved is a complex of interrelated values and principles which in the aggregate define the direction and character of the energy comprising the nation-state. The politician may be able to deduce and define with reasonable precision the interests of a state at a given time in history, in a given context and in the light of currently accepted general values for the state. But judgment concerning the adequacy or rightness of those general values of a nation-state requires a process more akin to aesthetics than to deductive logic or to the scientific method.

Furthermore, the values to be maximized are indeterminate as to time. They are not merely to be assessed over the immediate present or in their relation to some future point in time. They are to be integrated over an extended period including the present and the indefinite future. Looking back over other states in past historical eras, one should not assess the values actualized, for instance, by the Athenian city-state merely for their contribution to later civilizations, nor slight them because the Athenian city-state did not indefinitely survive. It is only reasonable to judge that the actualization of values by the Athenians had a component of worth in itself.

What has been said above with reference to the nation-state applies with perhaps even greater force to the values to be associated with Western civilization, with the free world, and most generally, with mankind of today and of the indefinite future. And the values associated with each of these are not identical with, although at many points they may converge with, the values associated with the United States as a nation-state.

VIII. THE ETHICAL FRAMEWORK

Earlier in this paper it was suggested that the concept "ethical framework" be distinguished from the concept of value systems associated with particular groups or even a limited system of interrelated groups. It was suggested that the phrase "ethical framework" be reserved for those approximate insights into objective value standing above earthbound value systems. Such insights, at a minimum, can be said to relate to the traditional idea of natural law; at a maximum, they can be said to relate to the insights of religion.

Being myself innocent of any theological training or discipline, I prefer to restrict myself to the minimum approach, that relating to natural law and philosophy.

I suggest that the following points have a bearing on the problem of finding some applicable content for such an ethical framework.

The first is the presupposition that the universe and that life are purposeful.

Professor Arnold Brecht of the New School for Social Research has recently re-emphasized the point that the entire structure of the scientific method depends on accepting the presupposition of consubjectivity, the acceptance of the real identity of an object observed by several persons. The scientific method cannot by its own method prove that consubjectivity exists. It accepts this presupposition on grounds of common sense.

That the universe and life are characterized by purpose similarly cannot be proved by the scientific method. The common sense grounds for accepting this ethical presupposition, however, seem fully as solid as those for accepting consubjectivity.

The second point is that the general direction of that purpose is not wholly beyond the insight of man. Common sense again rejects the proposition that if the universe is purposeful that purpose is trivial. It is possible to conceive of highly trivial conceptions and then of less trivial and still less trivial conceptions. A highly trivial conception, for instance, would be that the purpose of the universe is to maximize on a given day the production of bathtubs. A less trivial, but still basically trivial, conception would be that the purpose of the universe is to maximize the material satisfactions of mankind over the span of existence of mankind. If any distinction can validly be made between degrees of triviality, the general direction in which the non-trivial is to be found is, in principle, established.

Third, mankind has in the past developed non-trivial approaches to the question of the meaning and purpose of the universe and of life. The approaches by each of the great cultures have differed but none of them has been trivial. That of modern Western civilization—which has now spread to form at least a major component of the approach of most of the world—is based upon the accumulated experience, insight, and wisdom of the Judeo-Christian, Greco-Roman, and European cultures. One generation after another has added, adapted, tested for error, reconciled theory with practice and practice with theory. The resulting structure may be complex; it may not be wholly consistent; it may not be fully adequate to today's world; but it is not trivial. From it does emerge a sense of direction, an aid to understanding, a sense of the beautiful and an insight into values transcending those of individual, of class, of nation, of sect, or of generation—in other words, a framework of reason, of aesthetics, and of ethics.

The fourth point is that the human will can be effective only at the margin. Freedom is not absolute either for individuals or for nations. Much is determined by forces beyond our control, by events of the past which are irreversible, by accident or chance. At any given moment in time the margin of freedom left us may seem so small as to make it hardly worthwhile to exercise our will one way or the other. But the narrow margin of today becomes the foundation of the broader possibility for tomorrow. Over time the margin of freedom—of the possible—expands geometrically. The decision of today makes possible, or forecloses, ten decisions of tomorrow.

Fifth, the accumulated wisdom and experience of the past do not always give unambiguous precedents for decisions and actions at the relevant margin of freedom of the present. A new integration of general purpose with the concrete possibilities of the present may then become necessary.

Sixth, changes in degree may, at some point, move so far as to become a change in kind. The most difficult issues of foreign policy and ethics arise where changes of degree become so great that they cross this boundary line and fundamental changes in past policy seem to be indicated.

Let us examine a currently important foreign policy issue in the context of the ideas suggested above. Are any of those ideas relevant, and, if so, how and to what extent?

As an example, let us consider the circumstances, if any, under which the deployment and possible use of nuclear weapons might be justified.

Western civilization and its antecedent cultures have not taken the view that the precept of the Sixth Commandment was to be taken as an absolute. The values of achieving or maintaining freedom, diversity, and cultural growth and of combatting tyranny, reaction, and cultural stagnation or death have been generally considered to overweigh, at least under certain circumstances, the strong presumption against the taking of life. There has been much debate about the circumstances under which the important values are so threatened as to justify action involving the loss of life and much debate about what can be done to reduce the chances of such circumstances arising. But, except for absolute pacifists, the major point—that there may be such circumstances—has been agreed and has been the basis on which foreign policy has been conducted and judged from time immemorial.

There have been, from time to time, changes in the degree of destructiveness of weapons and of war. These changes have, up to now, generally been considered not to have invalidated the major point. But, with the advent of nuclear weapons in volume, we are faced with a new issue. Has the change in degree now become one of kind? At the extreme of the possible it may very well have become such. The release of the full potential for destruction of the nuclear weapons presently available in national stockpiles could amount to virtually total destruction.

Our consideration of an ethical framework suggests that the values, even the most important values, associated with any partial group of mankind, say the United States or the U.S.S.R. as nation-states, must be presumed not to be ultimate. A course of action likely to lead to general destruction cannot, therefore, be justified in support of those values.

That there are no conceivable circumstances under which the deployment and possible use of nuclear weapons would be justified does not, however, necessarily flow from the same premises.

The argument is made that the whole purpose of a policy of nuclear deterrence is to prevent nuclear weapons from being used. The thesis is that nuclear deterrence both makes possible the preservation of the values of freedom, diversity, and cultural growth and makes the general destruction of a nuclear war so unlikely as to make the risk tolerable.

Some would argue that no risk of so important a stake is tolerable. At a minimum it is clear that the risk must be reduced below its present magnitude. Can that be done? This is largely a question of fact rather than a question for ethical judgment. I believe it can, with great effort, be done—that by, say, 1965 we can so design and construct our nuclear defense system that no rational purpose could be served by the Soviet Union in initiating nuclear war and that, thereafter, little purpose would be served by either side in further accelerating the nuclear arms race. At such a time, if it has not earlier been possible, agreements on the control and regulation of armaments still further reducing the risk of nuclear war should, in my opinion, be possible.

An analysis of the reasons for the inherent instability in the current weapons confrontation between the U.S.S.R.

and the U.S. and the technical considerations which lead to the belief that this inherent instability can be radically reduced over the next few years is not appropriate for inclusion in this paper. The point relevant to this analysis is that an assessment of the facts, of feasible possibilities, and of probable consequences of alternative courses of action is an essential element in judging any important issue of foreign policy and ethics.

But the even more important conclusion is that the meaningful analysis of foreign policy cannot even be begun unless we have some idea of an ethical framework from which the analysis can derive its relevance.

"The Recovery of Ethics" was first published by the Church Peace Union (now Carnegie Council on Ethics and International Affairs), in 1960. Reprinted by permission.

CHAPTER II:

The Policy Process

Introduction

As the United States became more deeply involved abroad after World War II, improved coordination of national security affairs became a matter of the utmost importance. The principal milestone in the history of the postwar security structure was the passage by Congress in 1947 of the National Security Act. Though not directly involved in this legislation, Nitze nonetheless contributed to bringing it about. As vice chairman of the U.S. Strategic Bombing Survey in 1945-46, Nitze was chiefly responsible for synthesizing the project's findings, which, at President Harry S. Truman's specific request, included recommendations on the organization of the nation's postwar defense establishment. In its summary report on the Pacific war, published in 1946, the survey stressed the need for effective passive and active defense measures, up-to-date scientific research and development programs, improved intelligence capabilities to prevent another Pearl Harbor disaster, and unified direction and control of the armed forces—in other words, measures designed to cope with a divided and potentially hostile world in which future enemies might be armed with the most advanced military technologies, including nuclear weapons.[1] Similar reforms then under consideration in Congress eventually worked their way into the National Security Act, which among other things established a new organizational structure for national security, including an independent air force under a unified defense establishment, the Central Intelligence Agency, and the National Security Council to advise the president on the integration of high-level policy.

---

[1] See U.S. Strategic Bombing Survey, *Summary Report (Pacific War)* (Washington, D.C.: G.P.O., 1946), pp. 30-32.

In the selections that follow, attention is given primarily to the organizational and institutional aspects of policy-making. The first two essays discuss the role of the chief executive—the evolution and enlargement of his responsibilities after the war, and how presidents Nitze has known have shaped the machinery of policy-making to suit their particular needs. The third and fourth papers address the closely related problem of providing the president with sound, authoritative advice and of focusing in one place responsibility for assuring competent staff work on presidential-level national security decisions—a function that Nitze argues should properly reside with the secretary of state.

Nitze's insights into the intricacies of policy-making derive in the main from his long and intimate involvement in the policy process. Instead of theorizing from abstract models, he draws on his rich personal experience to illustrate and explain how the policy process works and where improvements have appeared needed. But in the final analysis it is Nitze's contention that organizations and institutions must be adjusted to those who run them. The factor of ultimate importance, he argues, is making the system work in getting us from where we are to where we ought to be.

6. The Modern President As a World Figure*

(1956)

Dean Acheson tells a story about President Roosevelt, who having once served as Assistant Secretary of the Navy preserved a special affection for that service, and General Malin Craig, who was Army Chief of Staff before General George C. Marshall took over in 1939. General Craig used to go over to the White House from time to time to advise with FDR, to get his approval of budget requests for the Army, and to discuss his worries about the indifferent state of our military preparedness in those days. During these discussions the relative size of Army and Navy appropriations and the superior readiness of the Navy would come up from time to time. After one somewhat heated exchange which ended with FDR's rejection of General Craig's pleas, the general concluded the discussion by saying, "Sir, I accept your decision, but I wish that when you refer to the Navy you could find some pronoun other than 'we' and that you would not always refer to the Army as 'they.'"

---

*Since World War II American presidents have had to shoulder increasingly heavy and difficult responsibilities, especially in the exceedingly sensitive area of foreign affairs. By the mid-1950s, foreign policy had emerged as the single most time-consuming and important item on the president's agenda, due largely to the potential for conflict and a highly fluid political scene abroad. The central theme of this essay is the need for creative and effective presidential leadership to bring and hold together the anti-Soviet coalition and to supply the ideas and policies by which coalition members may pursue their common aims and aspirations.

91

This story illustrates the problem of duties of the American presidency in terms of the "we" for whom the president speaks and to whom he bears a direct responsibility and the "they" whom he must take into account but to whom he does not have a clear responsibility. The confusion between the "we" and the "they" is potentially present in all aspects of the president's duties as chief executive of the United States, but this confusion is particularly acute and fraught with danger in the president's inescapable role as a world figure.

Within the United States the presidential "we" must on differing occasions embrace one or more of the following groups—the Cabinet, the executive branch, the entire government, the president's political party, and the American people as a whole. Only great political skill will prevent the president from omitting from a particular "we" reference a group or groups of Americans who feel they should have been included. Statesmanship consists, in part, in a wise and judicious use of the terms "we" and "they."

In *The American Presidency* Clinton Rossiter lists two types of duties or roles of the president. Functions of the first type flow directly from the language of the Constitution and define his primary responsibilities to the citizens of the United States. These constitutional functions include his duties as chief of state, chief executive, chief diplomat, commander in chief, and participant in the legislative process. Responsibilities of the second type which fall upon the president are those which are not provided for explicitly in the Constitution. The clearest example of a nonconstitutional function is that of chief of his party, Republican or Democratic. The presidential function as party leader is the result of historical development within America and is now regarded as a wholly legitimate function.

LEADER OF THE WESTERN COALITION

The nonconstitutional responsibility of the president which produces the greatest difficulties is that of being the leader of the Western coalition. World developments have thrust this function on the American president, and for the most part its legitimacy has been accepted by the American people. But it raises serious questions for the president himself.

The president bears a primary responsibility to the American electorate and a less well-defined responsibility to the larger nonvoting constituency of the "free world." The tension between the primary and the more inclusive "we" groups is illustrated when the president deals with allies like Britain and France. In dealing with them he is at the same time the Chief Diplomat of the United States seeking to uphold the national interest and the leader of the Western coalition seeking to strengthen it against a common external threat.

When the president speaks or is quoted his words are news throughout the world because he is the leader of the Western coalition. Statesmen and common people weigh his words and try to figure out whether they are included in his "we" or his "they." When he discusses matters of war and peace are they included in the "we" group? Are their lives and interests being considered as part of the "we," as a potential "they," or merely as counters to be used to promote the interests of some other "we" group of which they are not a part?

It is probably impossible for the president to reconcile the conflicting claims of all the various "we" groups to which he bears responsibility to the complete satisfaction of the more extreme members of any of them. But it still should be possible to have an opinion as to some of the better and some of the less satisfactory ways in which the problem of the "we" can be dealt with by a modern president.

TOWARD DEFINITION

The president's responsibility to his broader constituency has been described in different terms. Clinton Rossiter calls him the "leader of a coalition of free nations." Others have referred to him as "leader of the coalition of the free" or "of the free world." Sidney Hyman calls him the leader of a "a concert of allied powers." Some simply refer to the president as "world leader."

What is the group and what is the relationship to which these phrases refer? Do they all refer to the same thing or do they refer to different things? Historically the words "coalition" and "alliance" have been used almost interchangeably. In so far as there has been a difference it has been that the world "alliance" more often has implied an arrangement between independent states involving treaty agreements, while the world "coalition" has tended rather to emphasize a consensus of attitude and approach to a common problem. In today's context the terms take on a sharper meaning. In my view, a significant distinction can today be drawn between "coalition of the free," "concert of allied powers," and what is implied in the phrase "world leader."

When the president talks about "the coalition of the free," whom should he include in the "we"? Who are the "they" threatening the "us"?

Some people tend to emphasize the inner-community aspects of coalition and to denigrate the external-defensive aspects. Among the inner-community aspects they include common religion or ideology, common cultural heritage, common aspirations or ambitions, or common interests in security and progress. Others assert that historically coalitions have generally arisen as the result of a common reaction to a serious and direct common external threat. They refer to the great coalitions which overcame France's drives for hegemony over Europe under Louis XIV and Napoleon, and those which overcame Germany's drive for hegemony under the Kaiser and under Hitler. Today they emphasize the defensive origins of the free-world coalition in the face of the Soviet Union's drive for world hegemony.

Obviously both inner-community and external-defensive elements are combined in some proportion in any international coalition, in any consensus or pulling together of people beyond national lines. But the weight of historical evidence favors the greater force of the defensive element in evoking the type of "we" consensus to which the word coalition is usually applied.

"Coalition of the free"

If we accept the analysis thus far it suggests the following meaning for the "coalition of the free." The "coalition of the free" refers to the common element in the attitude of all those people who feel threatened by the drive of the Soviet leadership for world hegemony and therefore feel that they are part of a common "we" seeking, perhaps by very diverse means, some other answer to their political future than acquiescence in this Soviet drive. If one accepts this answer, the term coalition has a broad but reasonably precise meaning. It then refers to an attitude of mind. It does not refer to alliances, treaties, blocs, or membership in any particular organization. It does not refer to governments or nations as entities but to one aspect of the attitude of people in those governments and nations. It may even include bodies of men and women in countries governed by Soviet satellite regimes who hate and fear those regimes and what they imply.

The term "coalition of the free" is not, of course, always used in this sense, but neither is any other term dealing with political matters ever used consistently in any one sense. To this extent all terms used in discussing politics are ambiguous. If we are to communicate broadly we still must use them, trying to make our meaning as precise as the context will allow.

If one accepts the definition here suggested, it is obvious that the word "free" contributes meaning to the phrase in only a limited sense. Until last year we certainly would have included the Yugoslavs within this meaning of "the coalition of the free," even though the Yugoslav government was under Communist leadership. Perhaps they should still be included today. We would include the Spaniards under General Franco, colonial powers such as England, France, Belgium, dictatorships such as the Dominican Republic, and various other groups politically organized in a great diversity of ways. The common denominator, the special meaning of "free" in this context, is freedom from Soviet control and a desire to work out a political future in some other way than subject to Soviet hegemony.

Obviously any such "we" group, any such consensus, is fluctuating. It depends in large measure on the immediacy and overtness of the threat posed by the "they" which has called it into being. If that threat relaxes, or appears to relax, then the multitude of other issues, contradictions, or diverse loyalties normally tending to divide the "we" group come to the fore and weaken or break the consensus.

Today there is real doubt as to whether the members of the Asian-African bloc now consider themselves really threatened by the Russian drive for hegemony and therefore have any substantial feeling left of constituting a "we" consensus with the West. Other issues and other "we" and "they" divisions have now come to the fore. Asian statesmen like Sir John Kotelawala of Ceylon find that domestic political support is withdrawn if they follow a foreign policy consistent with an attitude of "we" consensus with the West which thereby underemphasizes other locally more appealing issues.

In emphasizing the defensive element, the element of fear, which calls the consensus underlying a coalition into being—I do not want to slight the opposing element—the feeling of hope that the "we" group has some chance of resisting or defeating the force that is threatening it. When Macedon in the days of Demosthenes had so grown in strength that there was real doubt that a coalition of those threatened by Macedon could successfully resist, all Demosthenes' eloquence was of no avail in bringing the Greeks into a working coalition in time. They delayed getting together; they attempted to make deals. When some of them, the Athenians and the Thebans, finally did unite to make a stand it was too late. They were defeated and forever lost their freedom.

"Concert of Allied Powers"

It is in this context of the elements offering hope that if the consensus of the free-world coalition is maintained, this coalition (or some smaller "we" group within it) can successfully resist or defeat the common threat, that we may, I suggest, consider the problem of alliances, of a "concert of allied powers." Here we are dealing, however, not with an attitude of mind but with the relations between governments—treaty commitments and regional special-purpose organizations. Before considering the president's functions and responsibilities with respect to leadership of a "concert of allied powers" a few words may be appropriate on the subject of the purposes of alliances and some of the more difficult questions of alliance diplomacy.

Professor McGeorge Bundy has pointed out the variety of purposes and objectives which alliances can serve. Alliances can define a mutuality of strategic interests. Alliances can serve notice on the "they" that encroachment beyond a certain point will elicit a common response. Alliances can provide a legal foundation for planning and for action. Alliances can provide a symbol around which a pre-existing or developing consensus can be organized and strengthened. And they can be effective, or they can be ineffective, in accomplishing the purposes for which they are created.

Professor Bundy stresses the importance of a fundamental community of political interests as a precondition to an effective alliance. He also stresses the importance of a common harmonious over-all strategic concept.

An alliance to be effective must be based on something more than the changing and possibly ephemeral attitudes which characterize a coalition as broad and inclusive as "the coalition of the free." To accomplish any of the purposes suggested for alliances a degree of permanence and stability would seem to be necessary. If they really are to serve notice against encroachment or constitute a legal basis for longer-term planning or action or provide a symbol of real political force, alliances should not be dependent upon short-term variations in the immediacy or form of the external threat, they should not be subject to drastic amendment if there is a normal overturn in the domestic political leadership within one or more of the member countries, and they should not be based upon ephemeral or misunderstood considerations.

The fostering of the "coalition of the free" and the building of an effective "concert of allied powers" are then two separate and very different although related operations.

WORLD LEADERSHIP

To some extent the people of the United States, the countries participating in the alliance system, and those beyond the alliance system who feel themselves to be part of the coalition of the free, all look to the president of the United States for some clarification of ideas and policies which look beyond and over the current East-West conflict. Granted that we may today be engaged in a vast politico-military-economic-psychological chess game with a very dangerous and capable opponent for the very highest stakes, still there is the hope that somehow the rigors of the game can be mitigated, that it need not be played out to an ultimate decision with all the loser's, and many of the winner's, pieces swept from the board. And we look for a leader to express this hope for mankind, to suggest a general policy by which it may be realized. To a certain extent the ability of the modern president to give effective leadership at home and to the alliance and coalition depends on his fulfilling this additional function concurrently with his other responsibilities.

The group which the president has in mind when he addresses himself to this function must include mankind generally. The ideas and proposals he puts forward in this context must plausibly provide for the basic interests even of those on the other side of the East-West struggle. When the president addresses himself to this function it is natural for him to refer to the United Nations, the organization which symbolizes this aspect of people's aspirations.

Obviously, in expressing ideas which apply to a world-wide group, the president must expect to run into opposition both at home and from the Communist leadership. To some at home this is the furthest possible departure from single-minded devotion to the exclusive group constituting the people of the United States, before whom, in effect, the president has taken his oath of office. To the Soviet leaders, pretensions on the part of the president to world leadership are pure bombast, since they consider themselves the natural spokesmen for mankind.

President Eisenhower's speech "The Chance for Peace," delivered before the American Society of Newspaper Editors on April 16, 1953, was probably the most effective recent effort to fulfill this function of "world leader." But many other statements of modern presidents and secretaries of state are understandable only in this context.

THE PUSH OF FACTS

It can be argued that the entire conception of a function for the president in the field of foreign affairs other than that of Chief Diplomat is artificial or wrong or based upon a temporary emergency, an emergency created by the two World Wars, and that it should be the object of policy to get away from such a function as rapidly as possible. Certainly the theory of the presidency would be clearer and neater if the functions and powers of the president could be kept within the strict framework of the

Constitution and related solely to the United States as a united and exclusive group.

But the facts of the domestic political scene seem to have made necessary the involvement of the president in what the framers of the Constitution considered perhaps the greatest danger to the Republic, faction and party. It is today hardly possible to conceive of the president in terms other than as leader and chief of his political party. Indeed many believe that the evolution of our system of government should be in the direction of further party organization and discipline and a closer tie between the president and his party; in order to ensure both more effective limitation of the power of the president and greater responsibility on the part of the party.

Similarly, the facts of the international scene may require that the president continue to further a consensus of those determined not to surrender their liberties to the Communists, continue to provide leadership to a concert of allied powers, and, in order to do these things effectively, continue to associate himself with the aspirations of mankind.

If so, the task of handling his actions and his words in such a way as to give simultaneous leadership to an expanding circle of "we" groups, to manage the conflicts of interests and loyalties that necessarily arise among them, will continue to be one of the modern presidency's greatest burdens.

"The Modern President as a World Figure," is excerpted and reprinted from *The Annals of the American Academy of Political and Social Science*, Philadelphia, vol. 307 (September 1956), pp. 114-123.

7. Presidents and the Development of National Security Policy

(1978)

I propose to address the subject of the president and the development of national security policy, rather than the more narrow subject of the president and the military establishment. Rather than tie my remarks to any particular president, I shall try to give you my viewpoints of what has happened in this field over several administrations. And moreover, I shall talk to you from the standpoint of the fish. There is a change of optics when you look at things from under the water rather than above. And since in my own experience I have often been in the middle of events—if not necessarily submerged by them—I propose to address this broad subject form my own particular experience.

Let me start with the president and the development of national security policy. I have found a fascinating area for study to be the evolving and changing way in which our presidents have addressed the interface between foreign policy and military policy, what today we call national security policy. These changes have depended in part on the personality of each of the presidents. In part they have depended on the nature of the problems that the country faced during his presidency. In part they have been influenced by the pertinent organizational structure, either that which he had inherited or that which resulted from his own initiative. I will try to outline my impressions of the changes in the way national security policy was addressed during the last seven-plus-a-little presidencies.

I came to Washington in the spring of 1940 to work with Jim Forrestral as a junior, unofficial member of the

White House staff. By that time the problem facing the country was the prospect of our involvement in World War II. The object of policy had become the building of national unity, getting help to our potential allies, and preparing for the possibility of our massive involvement in war. Even though I rarely saw the president, his overwhelming, if somewhat unorganized, vitality was clear to everyone working in the White House. I had no sense that he relied on completed staff work, on the precision of the directives that he signed, on coordination between the concerned departments and agencies. He relied more upon Harry Hopkins for foreign policy advice than upon the State Department, more upon Sumner Welles than upon Secretary Hull, and as much upon Henry Wallace and Henry Morgenthau as even upon Sumner Welles.

On military matters, he seemed to rely directly upon the chiefs rather than upon the secretaries of the Army or the Navy. Toward the end of the war it was my impression that the best staff work being done in Washington on the interface between political and military affairs was in the international policy section of the operation and plans division of the Army operating under Abe Lincoln's[*] direction. Somehow an immense and hugely successful military effort was organized, coordinated with diverse allies, and a war won. To my mind what suffered from this largely personal, somewhat instinctive and ad hoc approach to national security policy by the president was not victory in war, which General Marshall, Admiral King, and General Arnold did so much to make possible, but the subsequent unhappy peace.

To turn now to President Truman, it soon became evident that the central problem facing his administration was the wholly unsatisfactory state of the world following the termination of hostilities. The State-War-Navy Coordinating Committee, though it did some first-class work, was hardly an adequate national security policy instrument. It was not until George C. Marshall became secretary of state that it became possible to begin to turn things about

---

[*]Brig. Gen. George Arthur Lincoln (1907-1975), who served after World War II on the West Point faculty and from 1969 to 1973 as director of the Office of Emergency Preparedness.

organizationally. After General Marshall returned from the completely frustrating Moscow conference in April of 1947, he directed the department to create the Policy Planning Staff to keep under continuous review our policy toward our longer-range problems, particularly vis-a-vis the Soviet Union.

In July of 1947 the unification of the armed services was resolved and the Congress enacted the National Security Act, which created the Department of Defense, the NSC, the NSRB and the CIA. Thus a more orderly procedure for dealing with national security policy became possible. During this same spring of 1947 President Truman authorized the Greek-Turkish assistance program, the Truman Doctrine, the signing of the Rio Pact, the reorganization of the bizonal administration in Germany and, finally, General Marshall's speech at Harvard offering the Marshall Plan for the economic recovery of Europe.

To my mind those years, rather than having been dominated by a single charismatic personality, were dominated by President Truman's sense of the dignity of the office of the presidency, by his unwavering confidence in his senior associates, in particular General Marshall, Dean Acheson, and Bob Lovett, and by his willingness to encourage the development and use of organizational support in the national security field. During this period the central staff work on national security policy tended to gravitate to the State Department's Policy Planning Staff working in close collaboration with the Joint Staff or the Joint Strategic Survey Committee. It was during this period that the first in a series of basic national security policy documents, NSC-68, was prepared. The NSC machinery was used primarily for coordination of final review and decision, not for the preparation of the analyses and recommendations.

II

When Dwight Eisenhower became President, his view of the principal task facing the country was somewhat different. The pace of new initiatives that characterized the Truman years appeared to have put too great a strain on psychological, political, and economic resources of the country. He thought it wise to moderate the pace, to press harder for an armistice in Korea, to seek less dangerous relations with the U.S.S.R., and to reduce defense expenditures. In the field of national security policy organization he looked directly to the NSC staff structure for the staffwork on NSC policy issues. He thus put more weight upon that structure than . . . I thought it could really bear. He sometimes delayed his personal involvement in the crucial issues longer than may have been wise. When staff work on politically important issues is done organizationally too close to the center of final authority, that staff work soon loses the cold, objective, analytical approach upon which I believe it should be based.

Earlier in the last month of the Truman administration, there was a project to carry centralized staff work even further. . . . Gordon Gray was the head of the Psychological Strategy Board and the thought was to recruit various staff people from the CIA, the USIA, and the services to be located in the bowels of the White House or the Executive Office Building and issue instructions to the secretary of state, to the secretary of defense, to the service secretaries, and to the secretary of the treasury in order to coordinate the psychological impact of all the actions of the U.S. government on the foreign scene. This seemed to me to be a complete separation of authority from responsibility because these people were to be unknown, to be secret, to be invisible to the world and still to be able to tell the secretaries of the major departments what to do. Well, we succeeded in killing that project.

III

President Kennedy took a more youthful, dynamic approach than President Eisenhower. He was impatient with the NSC staff system as it had evolved. He did not believe in the utility of the annual Basic National Security Policy documents which had absorbed so much interdepartmental effort during the Truman and Eisenhower years. He abolished them. . . . He substituted the EXCOMM for most of the NSC work, the membership of which fluctuated with the issues involved. The staff work on national security policy became, to my view, somewhat unpredictable. His method of operation did give a greater lift and imaginativeness to national security policy, but it had its failures as well as its successes in execution.

President Johnson's years, as far as national security policy was concerned, were dominated by the Vietnam War. The NSC process initially worked reasonably well during his administration. The considerations for and against further involvement in Vietnam were, I thought, fairly well laid before the President. At a fairly early point in his administration, however, the situation had so evolved that there just weren't any good answers. I personally thought the decisive turning point came when President Johnson was unwilling to urge the Congress to increase taxes to avoid the inflationary aspects of the growing costs of our involvement, or to grant him more flexible authority to call up reserves. His unwillingness to amend the draft procedures so as to make the requirement for military service fall equitably on all our youths, rather than give effective exemption to those able to go to college and on to post-graduate work, further worsened the situation. He believed, perhaps correctly, that if he were to bring such issues before the Congress the debate would become a general debate on the advisability of continuing the Vietnamese War and that, he felt, he could not afford.

Thereafter, year by year, the potentially disastrous consequences of all the practicable courses of action became clearer and clearer. As the problems increased in difficulty, the NSC machinery worked less and less well. The focus of decision gravitated away from inter-departmental analysis and coordination prior to submission of recommendations to the president. The decisions were made directly by the president during discussions at the Tuesday luncheons or through similar more or less ad hoc procedures. The president, in my view, spent an inordinate amount of his time talking on the phone to outside advisers such as Abe Fortas and Clark Clifford. I'm talking about the period before Clark Clifford became secretary of defense. I found President Johnson to be a man with great drive, humanity and depth of sensitivity, struggling with too large an ego and too little solid confidence. He needed to dominate those around him and those who could really be helpful to him would not let themselves be wholly dominated. He thus came to rely on those not worthy of his own stature.

IV

This brings us to the presidency of Richard Nixon. I think he correctly evaluated the problem facing the nation as growing disillusionment with the Vietnam War domestically, a general weakening of our relative strategic military position and capabilities vis-a-vis the U.S.S.R., a worsening of our economic position relative to Japan and the OECD, and a loosening of our ties to our allies and friends. Under these circumstances, it appeared necessary to work our way out of the war in Vietnam, to normalize our relations with Mainland China and to work toward a policy of detente with the U.S.S.R., while trying to resist those at home and among our allies who wished to get away from confrontation as fast and with so little care for the consequences that we would have irrevocably turned control of the future over to our adversaries.

He found in Dr. Kissinger the indispensable collaborator for his purposes. In the fall of 1968, after the election, all the brighter young men who had experience in doing staff work concerned with national security policy were crawling over each other competing for an opportunity to work for Henry Kissinger on the NSC staff. As I remember it, he accepted some 130 of them. There was no doubt then as to where the focus of national security staff work was to be. The State Department Policy Planning Staff, ISA, the Joint Staff, ACDA, were each used almost entirely for technical inputs. At one time Kissinger referred to the entire network of subordinate echelons, including the secretary of state, the secretary of defense, the Joint Chiefs of Staff and the SALT Delegation as the "seventh echelon."

As it turned out, Kissinger's brilliance did not include the ability to get the best out of a large, highly intelligent but somewhat independently-minded staff. All but a very small number resigned or drifted away. Two or three moved over to the State Department when he became secretary of state but it can hardly be said that either in the handling of domestic affairs or in the handling of national security affairs was President Nixon supported by the quality of staff work which General Marshall had envisaged as being available to support the president of the United States.

When Gerald Ford assumed the presidency, he faced the domestic as well as the foreign problems left behind by the disasters of the Nixon debacle. I believe he saw the task as that of restoring domestic confidence in the institutions of government, of holding the country together economically and of fending off foreign dangers as best he could. In doing so, I believe history will give him high marks. Gradually the integrity of national security staff work was improved. I would give Jim Schlesinger, Donald Rumsfeld, and Jim Wade high marks in this effort. Rome cannot be rebuilt in a day but much good work was done.

"Presidents and the Development of National Security Policy" by Paul H. Nitze is reprinted with permission from *Evolution of the American Military Establishment Since World War II*, Paul R. Schratz, ed., (Lexington, Va: George C. Marshall Research Foundation, 1978).

8. "Impossible" Job of Secretary of State*

(1957)

President Eisenhower in a recent press conference described the position of secretary of state of the United States as "the greatest and most important job in the world."

When the President made this statement his main purpose undoubtedly was to emphasize his personal support for John Foster Dulles at a time when Mr. Dulles was under serious attack in the Congress and elsewhere. Furthermore the President probably did not mean to suggest a comparison in greatness and responsibility between the office he himself holds and that of his secretary of state. Nevertheless, the description is not to be lightly dismissed. A strong case can be made that the office of secretary of state of the United States is a more difficult office to fill well than the presidency—that, if not the greatest, it is the world's most difficult job. The most important exercise of the president's power and responsibility, provided he decides not to do the job himself, is his choice of secretary of state.

Clausewitz makes the point in discussing military organization that a supreme commander can lead, direct, and supervise eight to ten intermediate commanders, but that

---

*Compared with previous presidencies, Nitze found the Eisenhower administration top-heavy with unproductive and unresponsive policy machinery, most of it connected in one way or another with the National Security Council. Rather than abolish this machinery, however, Nitze favored giving it greater cohesion. He concluded that what was needed as a first step was a secretary of state with wide-ranging authority to act decisively on the president's behalf.

each of these intermediate commanders should not be assigned more than four subordinate units. His explanation was that an intermediate commander must look up as well as down, that he must concern himself as much with his relationship to his commander as with his relationship to his subordinates, and that the number of units he can therefore direct is more limited than in the case of the supreme commander who needs only to look down.

The relationships with which the secretary of state must concern himself are many, but probably the first and most essential is that with his immediate superior, the president. The powers and responsibilities with which the secretary of state is dealing derive almost entirely from those of the president. He acts in the president's name with authority delegated from the president or else the president acts in his own name but on the advice and recommendation of his secretary of state.

Any lack of understanding or of confidence between the two is a flaw that will rapidly undermine all possibility of successful conduct of the secretary of state's office. When President Roosevelt ignored Secretary of State Cordell Hull on vital matters of foreign policy, Hull's usefulness as secretary of state was seriously impaired. When Secretary of State James F. Byrnes slighted his obligations to keep President Truman fully informed and allowed doubt to arise as to whether he was fully reflecting Truman's wishes his usefulness as secretary of state was at an end.

But this relationship "up"—to the source of his power and authority, to the office in which the responsibility for his actions and those of all his subordinates is centered—is only one of the many relationships that the secretary of state must simultaneously cherish. To the 25,000 members of the State Department and the Foreign Service the secretary is the man in whose name and on whose responsibility all their actions are taken. A secretary who permits lack of confidence, or misunderstanding, to arise between himself and the organization of which he is the head soon finds himself in a very weak position.

In his first speech to the State Department employees after he took office Mr. Dulles said he could take personal responsibility only for those matters of which he had personal cognizance. But it is impossible for the secretary of state to divorce himself from responsibility for what the organization as an organization does. He cannot possibly do everything himself. He must, to a large extent, rely on others. He cannot avoid concerning himself with the competence and morale of the organization on which he and the president must rely for much of the development and execution of their policies. In this role the secretary of state must be an executive, the second most important executive of the executive branch of the U.S. government.

The secretary of state must concern himself with two other sets of relationships of the utmost importance. One of these is internal, within the United States, and finds its most critical expression in the secretary's relations with Congress, particularly the Senate. The other is external, the secretary's relations with the governments and people of the countries with whom the United States is allied or who are otherwise important to the conduct of our foreign policy. Both of these relationships are in part direct and personal, and in part dependent on public opinion and thus on all those things that help to mold public opinion, including the press.

During the years that Mr. Dulles served as special adviser to the secretary of state in the Truman administration he had an opportunity to watch at first hand the development of these relations under Dean Acheson.

It was my impression that Dulles found little fault, and in fact much to praise, in the way Secretary Acheson handled his external relations, particularly his relations with the leading men of the countries allied to us or uncommitted to either side. Dulles did, however, question Acheson's success in handling his internal relations, particularly his relations with Congress and the press. It was Dulles' view that the mounting bitterness toward Acheson on the part of an important segment of Congress and the press was destroying his ability to carry out the courses of action on which he was embarked and therefore undermining his usefulness as secretary of state. Dulles was determined not to repeat what he considered to be Acheson's errors in handling Congress and the press.

The question remained, and still remains, whether it is possible for a secretary of state simultaneously to maintain the good will of Congress and of the press, and also maintain the respect and confidence of our allies and friends abroad.

There are those who believe that the job of the secretary of state as it has evolved in the last twenty years is an impossible job. They say that one can conceive of a man—a first-class executive and leader of men, an expert in the field of foreign affairs—who is able to serve both as a loyal and dedicated staff officer to his president and as an executive and leader to his subordinates. They further say that it is possible to visualize this man conducting our foreign policy in a manner that merits and secures the respect of our friends and allies abroad and the fear and respect of our enemies.

But, they say, to imagine that this same man can also manipulate, weave through, accommodate and placate the myriad pressures, prejudices and opinions that are to be found in Congress, the press, and domestic public opinion is just asking too much.

Some have suggested that what we need is a secretary of state who has been through the domestic political mill, who has been elected to high office—either to the Senate or to a governorship—and who, because of this experience, will be better equipped to deal with the domestic scene and with Congress than any of our recent secretaries of state have been. They argue that the secretary of state, to be effective, must have domestic political power in his own right. They do not argue that experience and success in domestic politics are, by themselves, enough to qualify a man to be secretary. They urge that he have this background in addition to all the other qualities necessary for him to carry out well the demands of his job.

Others would question whether such paragons exist. They suggest that a choice has to be made, and that priority should be given to those qualities of character and experience which best fit a secretary of state to deal effectively with people and governments abroad. After all, the prime business of a secretary of state is the effective conduct of our foreign relations.

What are the qualities of character and experience that best qualify a secretary of state for this part of his job, the guidance and conduct of United States policy in what the Supreme Court once called "this vast external realm?"

I think most observers would probably list courage at the top of the list of essential qualities. The conflicting pressures on a secretary of state are so intense, the issues he is dealing with so important, and the merits, costs, and dangers of any course so difficult to sort out, that unless he has by innate character a disposition to energy, fortitude, and consistency—in other words, courage—his guidance of foreign policy will fluctuate and be uncertain.

In addition to consistency of policy, it is important that the policies pursued have a reasonable prospect of success, that they be based upon actual conditions and possibilities and not on prejudice, bias, or lack of understanding. The secretary of state is assisted by the full organization of the Foreign Service, by the State Department staff in Washington, and by the various intelligence agencies. They collect, digest, and evaluate information from a myriad of sources but, in the last analysis, it is the secretary who must decide on the final evaluation or recommend such a decision to the president.

This kind of judgment requires something more than experience. It requires a particular sensitivity, a power of intuition, an ability to put one's self into another person's place to see how a given course of action will appear not just to representative Americans but to people abroad—some friendly, some hostile, all human beings, but all having somewhat different backgrounds from ourselves.

Combined with this sensitivity, a secretary of state has to have somewhat the same capacity for toughness as a military commander. A general cannot hesitate to send a unit into an action that will almost certainly result in its destruction, if that action is necessary to the success of his over-all strategy. From time to time, a secretary of state is called upon to make decisions requiring a similar toughness of spirit. He is in no position to give orders to any foreign citizen or official; therefore this toughness often finds expression in a well developed ability to say no, but it is toughness nevertheless.

If one were to ask foreign observers, observers basically friendly to our interests, what quality in a U.S. secretary of state is most important, I believe they would say honesty. A reputation for honesty has long been stressed by students of diplomatic history as being the key to success in diplomacy and statesmanship. It is not that the diplomat or statesman should be a blabbermouth or have no secrets. It is that the statesman and the diplomat are presumed to have considered their remarks before they make them, to be precise in giving expression to their thoughts, and to mean what they say.

Even in negotiations between basically hostile states a high degree of precision in expression is necessary if misunderstandings leading to consequences desired by neither side are to be avoided. In the conduct of alliance diplomacy and particularly in the case of a nation that plays a role of leadership in a coalition or system of alliances, precision of expression and a reputation for honesty are absolutely essential.

It is important at this point to draw a distinction between that precision of expression which one finds in the fine print of a legal contract and precision of expression which conveys in a politically significant manner the meaning one intends. Henry L. Stimson, when he was secretary of war, was asked to approve a statement that his staff had prepared. When he objected that it was unclear, members of his staff pointed out that all the points he had in mind were covered somewhere in the language they had prepared.

His reply was that in the world of politics one should never forget that any public statement is to be judged as though it were a poster, not a photograph. The overall impression, not just the detailed words, must correspond with the thought that is intended.

It would be wrong, of course, merely to stress honesty and precision of expression without regard to the content of what the secretary of state wants to express. People abroad are fundamentally interested in two questions. The first question is whether we in the United States consider them to be part of the group in whose behalf we are conducting our policy of leadership, or whether we view them as mere counters to be played this way or that in a game in which they really have no part.

The essence of leadership is to promote successfully the basic interests of those one is attempting to lead. If the developing course of history has thrown on the United States the burden of leading a coalition of those who do not wish to accept Soviet hegemony in the world, then the secretary of state must have a sufficiently broad point of view to associate himself with the basic interests of the members of that coalition. He must be tough in saying no to those who would have him espouse interests that are partial and are not basic. Interests that really are vital to the members of the coalition must be vital to our secretary of state, and to us, if we propose effectively to lead the coalition.

The second question in which people abroad are interested is whether as a country we have the will and the determination to carry out the policies that we purport to be pursuing. A secretary of state who promises more than he can deliver debases the currency of our prestige as a country. Every concrete success of our foreign policy tends to improve our chances of further success. The close balancing of stated objectives with capacity for performance is an art that the secretary of state must constantly have in mind.

Our ideal secretary of state, then, is a man of many and seemingly contradictory virtues. He is a loyal subordinate to his chief while he is a leader and executive of the State Department and Foreign Service. He is courageous, and he is sensitive. He is honest, and he is precise and careful in his expression. He is broad-minded, and he is tough. He must be proud and he must be humble. Without pride, he would be unable to face the responsibilities that press upon him. Without humility, he would crack under strain.

In practice no actual secretary of state will fully meet our ideal. He will have great strengths and he will have weaknesses. The task of good government organization is to make it possible for human beings to carry superhuman responsibilities. The president, the White House staff, and the leaders of the political party in power can carry a major part of the burden of protecting the secretary of state from unfair congressional pressure and criticism.

The State Department and the Foreign Service can assist the secretary of state to the limit of their ability in the actual formulation and conduct of policy. Our friends abroad are willing to do what they can to help if given a chance. It is only as a team that the job can possibly be done at all. The secretary of state must permit—and help—the other members of the team to help him. Personal diplomacy is not enough. But even if he seeks and receives the fullest assistance others can give him, the unavoidable pressure of responsibility and burden of decision upon the secretary of state makes his job, if not the greatest, probably the most important, and certainly the most difficult in the world.

"'Impossible' Job of Secretary of State" is reprinted from *The New York Times Magazine*, February 24, 1957.

9. The "Vicar Concept"*

(1960)

Mr. Chairman, . . . the topic is the problem of gearing up the government for effective foreign policy and defense policy. It is always with us—a problem never solved with finality.

These realms of policy do not differ from purely domestic policy in respect to purpose and controlling principles. All policies of this government are supposed to

---

*While appearing in 1960 as a witness before Senator Henry M. Jackson's subcommittee on national policy machinery, Nitze added a further refinement to his concept of governmental responsibility—the idea that in all matters relating to the formulation and execution of foreign and defense policies, the president should look to his secretary of state to act as his "general managèr." Similar procedures were everyday practice in business and industry; it occurred to Nitze that they might work effectively in government as well. The model he had in mind was the relationship that had existed before Secretary of State Dean Acheson and President Truman. Nitze's apparent intention was to reinstitute a comparable partnership as the surest means of strengthening and clarifying lines of authority and responsibility. But while the general manager or "vicar" concept has been generally applauded since Nitze advocated it, opportunities for putting it into effect since Truman's day have been rare. Those who have tried, such as Secretary of State Alexander M. Haig, Jr., may not have fully understood what Nitze had in mind and, as a result, have often felt frustrated in trying to exercise such a role. The concept will only work if the president believes it to be sound and the secretary of state understands its limits.

be informed by the great purposes of the state laid down in the preamble of the Constitution. What distinguishes foreign policy and defense policy—the specific concern to this subcommittee—from the domestic policy is a matter of jurisdiction. Foreign policy and defense policy are directed toward the world environment. They reflect the national will toward matters lying beyond our jurisdiction. In that realm the government does not exercise ruling authority. It cannot quite lay down the law. It can at best only influence events and circumstances, not ordain them. Other wills are at work. They stem from premises and focus on purposes often different from our own and quite often not merely different but inimical.

This basic, simple characteristic makes foreign and defense policy more chancy and speculative and sometimes more exasperating than domestic affairs. While the inherent character of these realms of policy sets limits on what can be accomplished by planning, it also makes important and essential that we muster all the foresight, intellectual rigor, and circumspection that we can.

It is for this reason that I, among many, welcome the efforts of this subcommittee in developing a greater consciousness of the nature of policy in these fields and the problem of so organizing as to make possible our best performance.

There are dangers of oversimplification in any discussion of this subject. Analysis inevitably produces some distortion. One makes nice distinctions between policy formulation and operations or between command and staff functions. One draws neat charts dividing responsibilities into geometrically precise compartments. One speaks of levels of authority as if government could be arranged with the measured symmetry of a staircase. For analysis we divide things up; in practice they are all of a piece together.

Another set of difficulties arises. The precepts of sound policy and sound policy-making boil down to a set of maxims of copybook clarity—concepts indisputable and obvious. One is likely to say of them that the principles are mere matters of common sense, that everybody knows them. In a way this is true. Yet I think also that something which Clausewitz said of warfare is applicable here. He said that the important things were all simple and that the simple things were most difficult. I am sure that there is nothing recondite about sound policy-making. On the other hand, putting the simple precepts into practice in a government is an enormously exacting task. It requires sustained and rigorous application and unremitting exercise of authority and intellect. Discipline and order within a governing apparatus have to be created anew continuously.

My own way of getting at the problem is to divide the field of policy according to the breadth and the duration of the ideas involved.

I would begin with the enduring end of U.S. policy toward the world external to our fiat. It is to maintain and to enhance conditions in the world environment favorable to the survival, as political realities within our domain, of the precepts and values chosen and asserted in the foundation of our nation. This is the constant purpose. What it entails varies from one historic phase to another.

What it entails in any one phase might be called our national strategy. This strategy must be recast from epoch to epoch. To do this requires encompassing judgments and broad decisions which set the tone and establish the general premises of our undertakings in world affairs.

You may ask for examples. I suppose the first one in our national history was the decision to venture into independence, the decision that the Americans would constitute themselves as a nation, work out their own history, and deal with the external world in their own right. A second, surely, was the early decision to establish a base of continental scope. A third was the great decision asserting the inviolability of the American hemisphere.

More recent decades give us other instances: the decision recognizing the threat to us explicit in the ambitions of the Axis and determining to counter that threat; the decision to bring and to relate ourselves to an organized pattern of international responsibility in the sequel to World War II; the decision recognizing the true nature of the threat inherent in the power and thrust of communism and of the necessity of countervailing action.

How are such decisions arrived at? One may often pinpoint their emergence in some specific pronouncement such as Washington's Farewell Message, President Monroe's message which marked the origin of what has come to be known as the Monroe Doctrine, or, to take a recent instance, the Truman doctrine. These specific, clear acts are certainly great sources of policy. They are also, however, results of policy-making. They were not struck off as sudden, original acts without antecedents. They emerged from great interplay of forces and ideas and hard consideration within administrations, between administrations and the Congress, and between governing institutions and the public. I know no way of reducing to a graph or to any neat formula the complexities that go to make up the great decisions of policy which in turn serve as the bedrock on which still further structures of policy are erected.

Take one decision which is rarely commented on: The decision which grew out of the experience of the Korean war to involve ourselves specifically and concretely by the continuing commitment of U.S. military forces to positions on other continents.

Parenthetically, it is noteworthy how often this aspect of the Korean struggle is overlooked. The tactical frustrations of the fighting on the Korean peninsula are dwelt upon almost to the exclusion of consideration of the great strategic decisions of global importance accompanying that struggle and essentially related to it.

What I wish to emphasize here is merely the elusiveness and complexity of these great decisions. They were of historic import. Yet, from what I know about the processes producing them, I should find it most difficult to identify the moment when it will become resolved, or when multifarious forces converged to produce one clear stream of action, or to say that this or that was the procedure by which it was accomplished.

What I would stress here is the fallacy of the idea—however much I find implicit in much that is said and written about policy—that the great decisions are matters requiring only periodic attention.

Decision in this field is not like buying a new car. It is not a case of giving heed to the requirements at stated intervals—making up one's mind on what model to get and then putting the matter out of mind until the thing becomes worn out or outdated by changes in style. The requirement is for unremitting hard work. The great decisions can be made adequately only in consequence of a great many contributory determinations.

The articulation of our national strategy by no means exhausts the formulation of policy. The attitudes, appreciations, and the will to act reflected in the major strategic determinations must take form in wide arrays of policy undertakings. Auxiliary actions to give effect to our main intentions must be determined upon. Particular situations making demands upon our capabilities arise, and old exigencies decline—often in consequence of actions we ourselves have taken.

The allocation of resources among our purposes must be continuously reappraised and modified to suit circumstance. Specific policies must be refreshed in response to surges of change in an ever-fluctuating environment. Demands arise from political changes within and among other political entities, from shifts in their economies, and from the dynamic of invention. New means have to be devised for emerging situations. Our own schedule of priorities for action must undergo continuous reexamination so as to make the best use we can of what resources we can bring to bear.

So, to recapitulate, our policies have an enduring end. What this enjoins upon us, phase by phase, must be decided on in major strategic determinations. In keeping with these, a host of lesser and more particular decisions have to be made and actions taken—narrowing down to matters of mere detail and matters of limited and passing significance. Yet I would warn against any attempt to classify decisions according to any fixed scale of importance. There are great fluctuations in importance and difficulty among particular facets of policy from one phase to another. Problems have a way of blowing hot and cold—rising and falling in their criticalness, passing along on the escalator of importance both upward and downward. What are marginal problems in one phase may become central problems in another and vice versa.

Obviously, one characteristic of a properly functioning government is that problems should always get to the proper level of authority for decision—proper according to a sensible notion of who should be deciding what and of the criteria for decision. This is something so easy to say and so very difficult to insure. Things go wrong when the level of the deciding authority fails to match the intrinsic importance of the things decided or when the criteria by which decisions are resolved are too narrow.

Obviously a proper economy of authority requires not only that decisions be recognized for their inherent significance, passed to a sufficiently high level of responsibility, and decided according to the fitting criteria, but also that the time of those in the high places of authority should not be squandered on questions of inferior importance. This is elementary.

Now there is no final formula for determining the ratios of importance among problems and assigning them to various levels in the hierarchy of authority—the question can be worked out only through constant superintendence.

The other main principles of sound policy-making can be reduced to similar simple statements of the obvious. The strategic concepts should be in focus with the actualities of the exterior world and represent an adequate correspondence to the enduring purpose of our policies. Our broad undertakings should be commensurate with the strategic appreciation. The particular actions giving effect to these undertakings should be up to the mark—that is, adequate with respect to the intentions they are supposed to effectuate. Our means should be allocated among these intentions in accordance with some rational and realistic conception of the hierarchy of our interests and the range of our capabilities. All of it sounds so simple, and all of it is so endlessly exacting in practice.

If our problem were one of mechanics, we could devise our answers on charts, settle our difficulties by procedure, and keep things from getting out of hand by rigging up devices for balance and coordination. The trouble is, however, that our problems are not of this order. They involve another dimension—the factor of will. Empirical processes can tell us much about the nature of the world exterior to our jurisdiction and the forces operating in it, but they never complete for us the image of what these things are or the understanding of what we must do. What we must do flows, in part, from what we are. A study of the environment tells us the problems but never the answer for which we must strive. This must come from some inner dictate—from values inherent in our nationhood and in our concept of human dignity. The whole society is custodian of these values. The defining of what they impose on us in relation to our environment falls, above all and essentially, to the president.

The task of seeing that the major policies are all of a piece and that, taken together, they are congruent with the strategic concept determined upon requires continuous superintendence which only the powers of the presidential office can supply.

I do not mean just an office. I mean also a man and his full attention. The appreciations necessary to the strategic conception which is the basic element of our policy cannot be achieved by intermittent attention. They cannot emerge from briefings designed to reduce all complexities to a nutshell. They cannot be arrived at through policy papers designed to cover up dilemmas and smooth over the points of crux. The job cannot merely be distributed among subordinates.

If this central requirement of presidential leadership and executive energy is not fulfilled, it is difficult to the point of impossibility to redress the lack at other points. A thousand committees may deliberate, 10,000 position papers may issue, and the bureaucratic mills may whir to unprecedented levels of output in memorandums, estimates, and joint reports—but little will come of it all if the exercise of the central authority vested in the president is faltering, intermittent, or ambiguous. . . .

The task of seeing that the major policies form a consistent whole, congruent with the strategic concept determined upon, requires continuous superintendence that again must fall mainly to the president's responsibility. I would not, however, expect any president to do this alone. He will certainly require a vicar, a general manager, a chief of staff, for the foreign policy-defense fields. I believe that vicar should be the secretary of state. No committee can perform this function for the president. No council can do it. The role must be assigned to an individual— authorized, deputized, and recognized for that purpose. I believe he should have the backing of one of the line departments of the executive branch.

I know that it is a common practice to invoke the magic term "coordination." It is assumed that all that is required is to divide up the pie of responsibilities between the departments and agencies of government and then to direct that lateral coordination between them shall take place. I doubt that the problem is that simple.

The policy framework within which coordination is to take place is all important. Unless that framework is filled in first, coordination in foreign and defense policy becomes meaningless, even mischievous.

In this connection I shall quote from my colleague, Charles Burton Marshall:

> My ears pick up on hearing some new plan for coordination among, say, the political, military, and economic aspects of policy. What shall one call the preeminent function, the engrossing principle—as to which the elements of policy are

to be coordinated and to which they are to be subordinated—if not some political function or principle?

States relate to each other in many ways—the intimidatory or reassuring effect, one to another, of their capabilities for force; the interplay of their capacities to help or hinder or excel each other in production of goods and income; their influence on one another regarding the arts and training; the inter-change among them, or the withholding of organized knowledge about natural phenomena; and direct touch between governments through official channels and through the organizations created to facilitate interchange and collaboration. That list—military, economic, cultural, scientific, diplomatic, and organizational—is representative but not exhaustive. My question is: What is the political function if not that which encompasses, transcends, and interrelates all the other aspects? The political is the coordinating function, not a function to be coordinated.

A source of feebleness in our making of policy is that we have forgotten the preeminently and essentially political character of the state and have vainly expected coordination of policy to materialize without any sufficient political principle around which to coordinate its elements.

I do not mean to rule out committees and councils and the like. They are unequivocally necessary in running a government. Moreover, I am sure that the National Security Council as conceived in the National Security Act of 1947 is an adjunct of high utility to any president who uses it rightly—that is, as a forum of decision and not just as a papermill grinding through the motions of action without really acting or formulating apparent decisions that often do not decide anything.

I do not intend to dismiss the staff function either. Ideas must flow in both directions—up as well as down—in the channels of policy. The president, his secretary of state, and all the chiefs of the organs of policy concerned must always have the candid counsel and steadfast assistance of the best brains they can get.

This brings us to an old point of discussion: whether organizations or individuals count for most in this respect. It is a futile argument. I cannot imagine any organization functioning in the abstract without people to fill the slots. I cannot imagine individuals at work in this field without some understood and rational relationship among them. You must have good organization to get good use out of the right people. You have to have the right people to make even the conceptually best organization work. Good men will demand good organization or else leave. Good organization makes it possible to get and to hold onto the talents of good people.

It is well to remember that we are speaking of functions of government, and that that word comes from a Greek verb for operating a ship. That requires a man at the bridge with a destination in mind and a sense of direction. It requires a first officer who accurately reflects the master's intentions and estimates. Beyond that, the ship must be well organized and well manned. These are not two different things. It is not a question of which at the expense of the other. The two are mutually dependent.

The continuous reappraisal, the sensing of the exterior situation, the sensing of opportunities for action, the sorting out between the feasible and the infeasible in the realms of action, the anticipating of problems even before they emerge, and the recognition of those which have emerged for what they are—all these tasks integral to policy-making require mental exercise as exacting as any in human affairs.

It sometimes seems to me that the human attributes for this are the rarest and most highly required of all our needs. Yet in retrospect I often wonder at the richness of the talents available to the government. Whatever may be wrong with the situation in which we find ourselves, I am sure that the deficiency is not in respect to the spirit and skills of the people available.

Yet we should not take the attributes of the right human resources for granted. The component elements—here I draw on my own recollections of the public servants of true creative value I have known in the government—include, first of all, energy; sheer capacity to get hard work done. Second is acumen; the capacity to engage the mind with reality. Third is intellectual honesty. That is a moral quality involving a sense of devotion to truth, however painful and however at odds with what a superior may wish to hear. I recall a secretary of state who in a salutatory address to the Department, laid stress on what he called positive loyalty. I think something should be said for the importance of negative loyalty also—a faculty for shaking the head and saying no when that is what the situation demands.

These are the qualities to be sought, cultivated, and preserved in the channels of policy-making. Good organization is that which attracts individuals with such attributes and makes good use of them by giving them scope and opportunity to be heard. There are no formulas for this in terms of structure and procedures. It is mainly and essentially a question of the spirit which informs policy from the center of authority.

In conclusion I offer a few tentative ideas on organization for policy-making in this complex and difficult field.

(a) The organizational arrangements must be responsive to the president's will. He alone can know his own requirements and how they can best be met.

(b) It would seem to me to be normal and sensible if the president were to turn to his secretary of state to act as his general manager in the foreign field where diplomatic, military, economic, and psychological aspects need to be pulled together under a basically political concept. In this general manager capacity the secretary of state would have the responsibility of seeing to it that the significant questions and data were brought to the president's attention and that he was spared the necessity of squandering his time on the less significant issues.

(c) If the secretary of state has, or is given, this general manager responsibility, he will need a staff recruited, trained, and organized to help him in this policy development and coordination function. This function is quite different from that of diplomacy for which most of the Foreign Service is not trained.

(d) The National Security Council, the secretary of defense's office, perhaps the Joint Chiefs of Staff, and the Bureau of the Budget, under this organizational concept, would require staff people having general training and a point of view similar to that of the secretary of state's staff for policy development and coordination.

Thank you, Mr. Chairman.

Reprinted from the U.S. Congress, Senate, Committee on Government Operations, Subcommittee on National Policy Machinery, *Hearings: Organizing for National Security—The Department of State, the Policy Planning Staff, and the National Security Council*, Pt. VI, 86th Cong., 2nd Sess., May 26, June 17 and 27, 1960 (Washington: G.P.O., 1960), pp. 853-860.

CHAPTER III:

The Foreign Policy Component
Of National Security

CHAPTER III: THE FOREIGN POLICY COMPONENT
OF NATIONAL SECURITY

Introduction

In Nitze's view, the development of effective national security programs requires careful and close coordination of several major components. Foreign policy is of particular importance because it is perhaps the single most sensitive indicator of how the United States—or any country—operates in evaluating and responding to developments on the world scene. This includes both the *declaratory* policies that the country may adopt as well as the *action* policies it chooses to pursue. In other words, besides being the focal point of America's dealings with the rest of the world, foreign policy serves a most vital security function, providing the nation's first line of defense.

Though Nitze's views on foreign policy appear throughout this volume, the papers presented here are especially pertinent. The first two date from the early 1950s and are adapted from speeches in which Nitze endeavored to place in clearer perspective the many profound changes that had occurred in U.S. foreign relations since World War II. While discussing the various effects these changes have had upon America's role in the world, Nitze reminds us that some traditions are not easily discarded and that there are guiding philosophic principles, dating from the origins of the republic, that should continue to exercise a strong influence on shaping America's purpose abroad.

The remaining essays in this chapter are more closely focused, dealing in the main with a foreign policy problem unique to the American experience—the management of a permanent peacetime security alliance. With the creation of the North Atlantic Treaty Organization (NATO) in 1949, the United States shed its 150 year old aversion to involvement in so-called "entangling alliances." But as Nitze points out, the mere establishment of NATO was one thing; making it work has been quite another. Ever since NATO came into being, he argues, the central problem has been to devise a strategy for the defense of Europe that will present a credible deterrent to the Soviets and win support among the allies as offering viable alternatives should deterrence fail. From this perspective, he took exception to the exceedingly heavy reliance that the Eisenhower administration placed on nuclear weapons in the 1950s, and in the following decade emerged as one of the leading defenders of the flexible response doctrine that is still the official basis of NATO strategy.

10. The Seven Pillars of Unwisdom*

(1953)

Admiral Conolly. I have been looking forward to this opportunity to explore with you and with the members of the college some of the more general questions and considerations in the field of foreign policy. The questions mentioned in your letter are among the most knotty ones we have had to deal with in the Policy Planning Staff over the last few years. This whole field is now being restudied and re-thought by fresh minds under the new administration. This occasion offers me an opportunity to go over with you some of the underlying relationships as they have appeared to some of us more tired hands.

The approach which I propose to take may appear to be somewhat theoretical and analytic. In certain circumstances such an approach may clarify rather than confuse.

But to dive into the heart of the subject, I should like to start by discussing three interrelated concepts.

---

*In the spring of 1953, shortly before resigning from the Eisenhower administration, Nitze delivered this address to the faculty and students of the Naval War College in Newport, Rhode Island. The theme of the speech, stressing the need for a stable world order and for comprehensive and realistic policies for dealing with the Soviet Union, was one that Nitze would return to often throughout his career. But the manner in which he presented it here, downplaying the simplistic, single-factor solutions offered by some, sets Nitze's writings and public speaking apart from many others.

The first of these is the preservation of the republic, the second is the reduction of Soviet power and influence, and the third is the avoidance of war.

These three concepts, stated in various ways, appear explicitly or implicitly in almost every statement of our national aims. The way in which they are phrased is important; perhaps more important is the way in which these concepts are conceived of as being interrelated.

It has seemed to us in the Policy Planning Staff that the first of these concepts, the preservation of the republic, differed in kind from the other two. The concept of the reduction of Soviet power and influence is a contingent concept which depends from an external fact, the fact that today the principal threat to our republic comes from the power and influence of the Soviets. The third concept, the avoidance of war, is also contingent in that there clearly are circumstances under which we could not preserve the republic if we were unwilling or unprepared for general war.

It seemed to us, therefore, that the first concept differs from other aims, objectives, or policies. We thought a more useful and descriptive word to describe this concept was the word "purpose."

In one of the important National Security papers [NSC 68] prepared in the spring of 1950, we expressed it this way:

> The fundamental purpose of the United States is laid down in the Preamble to the Constitution: ". . . to form a more perfect Union, establish Justice, insure domestic Tranquility, provide for the common defence, promote the general Welfare, and secure the Blessings of Liberty to ourselves and our Posterity." In essence, the fundamental purpose is to assure the integrity and vitality of our free society, which is founded upon the dignity and worth of the individual.

I should like to emphasize three points about this formulation. The first is that it is tied into the United States Constitution to which, as servants of the American people, we take our oath of office. As such it is not wholly applicable as a statement of purpose applicable to the free world coalition.

The second is that it calls for more than mere survival. It calls for the creation of conditions in which our system can live and prosper.

The third is its emphasis upon our willingness to fight if necessary to defend this purpose.

Let us now take a more thorough look at the second concept we started with, the reduction of Soviet power and influence. In a certain sense this is merely another and narrower way of saying the creation of conditions in which our system can live and prosper.

At this point we are in the center of what we are usually talking about when we refer to foreign policy.

By way of introduction it may be useful to suggest a definition of foreign policy. Foreign policy can be defined as being the projection of the will of the State to matters external to its domain; in other words, the courses of action undertaken by a government to affect matters of concern to it but beyond the span of its jurisdiction. The concern and focus of foreign policy relate to matters beyond the span of its jurisdiction. Furthermore, foreign policy relates to acting—that is matching of ends and finite limited means.

Therefore, when we discuss as an aim the creation of conditions in which our system can live and prosper, or the reduction of Soviet power and influence, we are talking only about one aspect of the foreign policy problem. We are talking about aims without having as yet related them to the means which we propose to use in achieving them. And we are a long way from the concrete actions which alone can be expected to achieve them.

It is when we get to the third concept, the avoidance of war, that we begin to get into the field of the means which we propose to use in achieving our ends.

One of the principles the United States has stood for is that war should not be used as an instrument of foreign policy. Obviously a disagreement about trade policy, fishing rights, adequate compensation for the taking of property, unfriendly statements, or failure to ratify a treaty are not matters where the ultimate sanction of war is appropriate.

If the fundamental purpose of the United States is threatened, if we are faced with defeat or the real prospect of eventual defeat if we cannot preserve or achieve certain vital aims, this question takes on a different meaning.

The United States has considered that an attack on any of the American states, that an attack on the European states who are members of NATO, now including Greece and Turkey, that an attack on Western Germany, Berlin, or Japan, that an attack on the Philippines, Australia, New Zealand or on Formosa would constitute such a threat, and has registered this either by treaty or presidential declaration. We have gone further to give solemn warnings with respect to other areas, such as Yugoslavia and Indochina. We have gone into a limited war over an attack on the Republic of Korea.

The question remains, however, as to whether we should resort to general war against the U.S.S.R. in order to bring about a recession of Soviet power from the satellites and from China. It is this question which underlies much of the argument as to liberation versus containment.

In the same NSC paper to which I referred earlier, the policy of containment was described as follows:

> As for the policy of "containment," it is one which seeks by all means short of war to (1) block further expansion of Soviet power, (2) expose the falsities of Soviet pretensions, (3) induce a retraction of the Kremlin's control and influence and (4) in general, so foster the seeds of destruction within the Soviet system that the Kremlin is brought at least to the point of modifying its behavior to conform to generally accepted international standards.
>
> It was and continues to be cardinal in this policy that we possess superior overall power in ourselves or in dependable combination with other like-minded nations. One of the most important ingredients of power is military strength. In the concept of "containment," the maintenance of a strong military posture is deemed to be essential for two reasons: (1) as an ultimate guarantee of our national security and (2) as an indispensable backdrop to the conduct of the policy of "containment." Without superior aggregate military strength, in being and readily mobilizable, a policy of "containment"—which is in effect a policy of calculated and gradual coercion—is no more than a policy of bluff.
>
> At the same time, it is essential to the successful conduct of a policy of "containment"

that we always leave open the possibility of negotiation with the U.S.S.R. A diplomatic freeze—and we are in one now—tends to defeat the very purposes of "containment" because it raises tensions at the same time that it makes Soviet retractions and adjustments in the direction of moderated behavior more difficult. It also tends to inhibit our initiative and deprives us of opportunities for maintaining a moral ascendancy in our struggle with the Soviet system.

In "containment" it is desirable to exert pressure in a fashion which will avoid so far as possible directly challenging Soviet prestige, to keep open the possibility for the U.S.S.R. to retreat before pressure with a minimum loss of face and to secure political advantage from the failure of the Kremlin to yield or take advantage of the openings we leave it.

The continuing requirements of a program of gradual coercion without resort to general war are very great indeed. These requirements are in part economic. It is a very expensive business both for us and for our allies to build and to maintain for as long as may be necessary military power superior to that which the Soviets and its satellites have and are building. The political requirements in the form of fortitude and continued willingness to make real sacrifices for a slow-moving policy are also very great.

There is therefore continued pressure to find some quicker and easier road to the attainment of our objectives. This pressure finds its expression in a number of suggestions as the conduct of our foreign policy.

These suggestions group themselves into distinct categories. It was once suggested that we might call them the seven pillars of unwisdom.

The first pillar is victory through reorganization. The advocates of world government, Atlantic Union, sole reliance on the United Nations fall in this category.

The second pillar is victory through lung power. Those who believe that through threats, promises, hortatory speeches, or merely through the simple clear exposition of our aims the walls of Jericho will collapse, fall in this category.

The third pillar is victory through change of person-alities. In this group fall those who believe that the United States is inherently omnipotent and that insofar as there are problems in the world they must spring from the incompetence or treasonableness of individuals. If we were to remove them, our problems would fall away.

The fourth pillar is victory through eliminating our allies. This group believes that the sins of the British or the French, or some other foreigners on our side, are so corrupting our position that if we could eliminate them and pursue a pure United States foreign policy victory would be easy.

The fifth pillar is victory through retreat. It being apparent that our commitments exceed our capabilities, assuming that we are not to increase our present efforts, it therefore follows that we should withdraw our commitments even if this means going back to the Western Hemisphere.

The sixth pillar is victory through personal diplomacy. If we only had people competent to talk turkey to our allies or to the enemy, or if those who are competent were permitted to conduct our diplomacy as their experience indicated, our problems would fall away.

The seventh pillar is victory through technology—or concentration on new weapons, particularly atomic weapons. This group tends to move over to the "drop the bomb now," or "we should have dropped the bomb earlier" school.

Now each of these points has in it an element of wisdom. It is only when the proposition is made that one can rely solely on a partial element and that it is not necessary to devote energy to other essential elements that one is led into unwisdom.

It is the last pillar, in variations of the "drop the bomb now" form, that presents the most serious issue of policy.

As vice chairman of the United States Strategic Bombing Survey I supervised the analysis of the effects of the atomic bombs dropped at Hiroshima and Nagasaki. These were 20 kiloton weapons with effects equivalent to one to two thousand tons of conventional high explosive and incendiary bombs. Present weapons can have far, far greater explosive power. Their probable effectiveness goes up somewhat less than the square of the cube root of the increase in power. In other words a weapon of 160 kiloton power will have approximately twice the radius and four times the area of destruction of a 20 kiloton weapon. A weapon of 80 kilotons will have a radius of destruction of 1.6 times, and area of destruction 2.5 times that of a 20 kiloton weapon or the effectiveness of, perhaps, 2,000-5,000 tons of conventional bombs.

A thousand atomic weapons each of 80 kiloton power would then have the effectiveness of 2 to 5 million tons of conventional bombs. During the last war 2.7 million tons of bombs were dropped on Germany.

I doubt whether anyone can be completely clear, were general atomic war to occur, as to the impact on the U.S.S.R.'s willingness and ability to continue war of such levels of destruction concentrated in a short time period.

There is also the question of the vulnerability of ourselves and our allies to present Soviet atomic capabilities.

Quite apart, however, from questions as to the decisiveness of an atomic attack in causing the U.S.S.R. to surrender, there are further questions as to the state of the world which would follow upon such a war and whether this would in fact create "conditions in which our system can live and prosper."

The answer to this last question in part depends upon the conviction of mankind generally as to whether the war was clearly forced upon us or whether it was undertaken by the United States as an instrument of an expensive national policy.

In any event it is the clear decision and pronouncement of both the last administration and of this administration that we propose to pursue our national aims by means other than general war.

To go back then to the three concepts that we started with, the preservation of the republic, the reduction of Soviet power and influence, and the avoidance of war, their interrelationship and hierarchy stands out clearly. The first one, the preservation of the republic, is at the heart of our fundamental purpose as a nation; the second one is an aim which is part of a wider aim, the creation of conditions in which the republic can live and prosper; the third one is a limitation upon the means which we propose to employ in achieving this aim. To put these three concepts in a hierarchy of relative importance the order would be preservation of the republic first; the avoidance of general war, second; and the reduction of Soviet power and influence, third.

As I mentioned earlier, policy is more than purpose or aims. It is intentions arrived at after taking into account both ends and means; it is most importantly actions undertaken to carry out intentions. In the field of foreign policy these actions are ones which project our national will beyond the sphere of our jurisdiction.

A clear understanding of our purpose and our aims and their hierarchy and interrelation is essential as a starting point for policy formulation. The really knotty problems, however, begin to emerge when one gets into the field of intentions. An aim does not become an intention unless one is prepared to allocate sufficient means to make its attainment probable. The usual position is that the means which we have at our disposal are inadequate to achieve concurrently all desirable ends. This is true whether the problem is one in the economic field, the military field, or the political field. Even the ends are often in some degree of inherent conflict. One then is faced with dilemmas and difficult decisions.

One of the more obvious issues of this type is constantly before us, the problem of the defense budget. It is obvious that a healthy United States economy is an important and extremely desirable aim. A balanced budget and reduced taxes are desirable in themselves and would contribute to this aim. It is also obvious that an increase in our military capabilities would be desirable. Even after all possible steps are taken to reduce the dilemma by greater efficiency by elimination of waste and duplication, an issue still remains which must be settled and decided in a way which does not wholly satisfy all desirable aims on the basis of judgment after the weighing of innumerable factors.

Similarly, in the political field we are met with dilemmas and issues which are complex and interrelated and where to some extent the lesser aim must be sacrificed for the greater on the basis of judgment. Such an issue was presented by the Arab states' proposal for the inscription of the Moroccan and Tunisian cases on the agenda of the

General Assembly.* It was perfectly clear that our position in the Arab world would be improved by voting for inscription. It was also clear that our position with the French would be improved by taking a firm line against inscription. It was also clear that nothing concrete would be gained by discussion in the U.N. On the other hand, the United States had consistently supported the position that the General Assembly should be available for the discussion of any matter of legitimate concern to its members.

After weighing all the considerations, the decision was made to abstain the first time the matter came up. By the time it came up a second time we had worked the position out with the French to a point where we could vote for inscription.

The entire process of allocating, rationing, and assigning resources, political, military, and economic between competing programs addressed to diverse but interrelated aims is of the essence of policy-making in the United States government.

I wish, however, to go back to a point I made earlier and that is that the real payoff is in action. It is in the skill and determination with which individual courses of action are executed that the real impact of the projection of our national will abroad is felt. It is in the bravery and skill of our officers and men in Korea, the care and imagination with which a speech such as the President's speech before the American Society of Newspaper Editors is prepared, the continuing patience and determination of our negotiators, to mention but a few examples, that the issue will be fought out.

---

*Reference is to demands by Morocco and Tunisia, in the wake of violent public demonstrations in 1952, for autonomy from France.

11. History and Our Democratic Tradition in the Formulation of United States Foreign Policy*

(1954)

Modern physicists emphasize what they call the theory of complementarity. They say that one can get a better insight into most of the problems of physics if one looks at them from more than one approach even though the approaches themselves may not be immediately reconcilable. Thus to get an insight into the nature of light one must consider it both from the standpoint of light particles or photons and from the standpoint of wave mechanics. Neither standpoint alone is adequate; the two standpoints are not fully reconcilable; both are necessary to explain the actual behavior of light.

Similarly it is sometimes helpful to look at our foreign policy from two different standpoints. One standpoint is that of our American traditions. The other is the world situation impinging upon us, the forces and peoples beyond our domain—forces and peoples having traditions generally different and sometimes diametrically opposite to our own.

---

*Speech at Boulder, Colorado, April 27-28, 1954. After leaving government in 1953, Nitze devoted considerable time and effort to studying the historical and philosophical underpinnings of American foreign policy. Out of his investigations came the following address which he delivered before the seventh annual Conference on World Affairs held in the spring of 1954 at the University of Colorado.

Both of these factors have a long and vital history. Both look to the future. The task of formulating foreign policy is the endless one of relating our actions both to our American tradition and to the facts of the external world.

I wish to stress certain general concepts informing our conduct rather than going into the particular mechanics of our practices.

The first informing principle importantly relevant to the formulation of foreign policy, it seems to me, is the principle that government derives its just powers from the consent of the governed. This is articulated in the Declaration of Independence. Though not spelled out in the Constitution, it underlies the whole document, since the Preamble embodies the notion of a people laying down the purposes for which government is created.

Certainly the idea was not an American invention. Our constitutional forebears derived it from European backgrounds.

The second informing principle is the protection of the individual and of minorities against arbitrary pressures from society.

Here again the concept is not one invented by Americans but one taken over from backgrounds abroad and applied with new vigor and completeness in the new start in life for which destiny gave the Americans rich opportunity.

The third is the separation and balancing of governmental powers, an idea which our constitutional fathers derived in part from Locke and Harrington and perhaps also from Montesquieu and then embodied in our Constitution.

The fourth is a decent respect to the opinions of mankind—a concept specifically expressed in our Declaration of Independence to reflect the consciousness of our national founders of our inherent responsibility as a people in a community embracing other peoples on other shores and their awareness of our relationship to other cultures antecedent to our own.

The fifth informing principle is the philosophy enunciated in the first amendment to the Constitution, which begins as follows: Congress shall make no law respecting an establishment of religion, or prohibiting the free exercise thereof.

Here the precepts of the Founders seem to have gone somewhat beyond theretofore established practices. What they laid down as a principle bridling the Congress was not general to the American polity in that day, for some of the component states still practiced and for some few decades continued to apply religious discriminations. The concept, however, had been brought over from Holland by Roger Williams and others many years before. The evolving influence of time has made the principle now a universal and fundamental one in our nation.

If one believes that there is something beyond man and history; that truth exists; that the human mind assisted by the spirit of free inquiry can, in some approximate but necessarily imperfect manner, approach to truth; that (to paraphrase the words of Jefferson) the duty we owe to our Creator can better be directed by reason and conviction than by force or violence, then not only freedom of religion but the other elements of our political philosophy flow reasonably enough. Then it is proper to protect the individual against arbitrary pressures even of the majority, then it is proper to separate and balance the legislative, the executive and the judicial functions, then it is appropriate to seek the consent of the governed, and finally to give a decent respect to the opinions of mankind.

Suppose on the other hand that one conceives a rulership as not only the embodiment of civil power but also of truth. Then these things do not follow.

That is what the Japanese did in their belief—brought into question only in the sequel to defeat in World War II—that the emperor is directly descended from the Sun Goddess, that he is not only the embodiment of the nation-state, but also the source of truth and destiny.

Analytically, Hegel does an equivalent thing in the doctrine that the nation-state is the highest embodiment of the idealist dialectic, and Marx does it also in the concept of dictatorship of the proletariat as the embodiment of the materialistic dialectic. Under these concepts, none of the conclusions I have enumerated follows.

If there is a union in the same hands of the sources of belief and the powers of government, certain things flow almost of logical necessity. The executive tends to dominance; the pressure of society on the individual with respect to all matters touching the corporate interests of the nation-state becomes overwhelming; the unquestioning loyalty, rather than the willing consent of the governed, is demanded and if necessary coerced; the opinions of mankind become of only secondary importance. History is replete with examples of the great military and political power that can be generated by states so organized.

The Frenchman Alexis De Tocqueville, a sincere and early admirer of our democratic system, was doubtful whether our system could be successful in other than a protected situation. He questioned whether countries less favorably situated could adopt a system such as ours. He thought that the principal European powers, because of their exposed positions, required a greater concentration of power in the national government than our system seemed to permit. He was particularly troubled by the fact that in the War of 1812 our federal government was unable effectively to call up the militia of Massachusetts and Connecticut for the defense of Washington. He also questioned whether the people of other countries shared widely and deeply enough that religious and philosophic background which seemed to him a precondition for our form of government.

A reasonable maturity of judgment, widely shared among its citizens, does seem to be a requirement for the preservation of a republic. This is the more so in that under our traditions and institutions many important issues, and in particular those arising in the area of foreign affairs, take on a more complex aspect than under a more centralized system.

Let us consider the elemental issue of patriotism.

The simplest and easiest formulation is obviously that given by Stephen Decatur in a famous toast: "My country, in her intercourse with other nations, may she always be right! But, right or wrong, my country!"

John Adams has given us a more complicated formulation: "In truth what is comprehended in the spirit of patriotism? Piety, or the love and fear of God; general benevolence to mankind; a particular attachment to our own country; a zeal to promote its happiness by reforming its morals, increasing its knowledge, promoting its agriculture, commerce and manufactures, improving its constitution and securing its liberties; and all this without the prejudices of individuals or parties, without fear, favor or affection."

I think he is right. If one believes in the philosophy underlying our Constitution and in the separation of the sources of religious belief from the powers of government then one's loyalties must take a more complex form than mere unquestioning allegiance to the state.

A second element which becomes complex under our democratic tradition is the relation between the executive and the legislative branch in the conduct of foreign affairs. The drafters of the Constitution were quite clear that external dangers to the state justify a higher degree of centralization of authority in the executive than do purely domestic issues. The president is made commander-in-chief of the Armed Forces. The chief burden of responsibility for the conduct of the foreign affairs of the United States also falls upon the president. But the power to declare war, to appropriate funds, to consent to treaties, to confirm appointments, and the power to investigate are in the legislative branch.

Under these circumstances the processes of the legislative branch, which are admirably suited to the compromising and reconciliation of the diverse sectional and group interests which underly the great mass of our domestic issues, become intimately involved in the formulation of foreign policy. In the domestic field, decisions once arrived at are reasonably final. They apply to an area over which the United States government has direct jurisdiction. Foreign affairs are by definition affairs over which the United States government does not have direct jurisdiction. They deal with an area in which the tools are negotiation and influence, where the passage of a law can authorize a course of action, or confirm the results of a negotiation but cannot in itself decide the issue.

Furthermore, the people themselves, under our system of government, must be enabled to form an opinion on how far—in a general way—they want their government to go on the crucial issues of foreign affairs. Against this background they must express periodically their preference as between the sets of leadership offered to them by our political parties.

For the people themselves to arrive at sound and reasonably informed judgments is easier with respect to domestic issues, with which we are all in daily touch, than with respect to the more distant issues of Europe, Asia, and even of Latin America.

Machiavelli deals at some length with the danger in democracies of the temptation to leaders to promise bold and courageous external policies at little seeming cost, even though grave risks to the republic are hidden in them.

History is replete with examples of the temporary popularity of such leaders and of the disasters which have ensued.

Such considerations, among others, led the drafters of our Constitution to provide, not for a pure democracy, but for a representative system, a system of checks and balances with a reasonably strong executive, especially in the field of foreign affairs.

But it still may be true that our particular institutions tend toward the wise handling of domestic issues rather than toward efficiency in world politics.

In the early days of our Republic, both streams of influence, the objective situation of this country in its relation to the world at large, and the stream flowing from the character of our institutions converged to dictate a policy of substantial isolation from world politics.

Washington's Farewell Address puts it this way:

> The great rule of conduct for us, in regard to foreign nations, is in extending our commercial relations, to have with them as little political connection as possible. So far as we have already formed engagements, let them be fulfilled with perfect good faith. Here let us stop.

Washington went on to describe Europe's primary interests as having no, or very remote relation to us. He observed that Europe "must be engaged in frequent controversies, the causes of which are essentially foreign to our concerns." Hence, he went on, "it must be unwise in us to implicate ourselves, by artificial ties, in the ordinary vicissitudes of her politics or the ordinary combinations and collisions of her friendships or enmities."

Washington saw "Our detached and distant situation" as inviting and enabling us "to pursue a different course."

"Why forego the advantages of so peculiar a situation?" he asked. "Why quit our own to stand upon foreign ground? Why, by interweaving our destiny with that of any part of Europe, entangle our peace and prosperity in the toils of European ambition, rivalship, interest, humor or caprice?

"'Tis our true policy to steer clear of permanent alliances with any portion of the foreign world."

But it seems clear that it was only because the two streams of considerations, the stream flowing from the facts of the external world and the stream flowing from our domestic institutions, converged that our Founding Fathers advocated such a policy. Consider for instance Jefferson's comments to Livingston just six years later on the subject of the Louisiana Purchase:

> The day that France takes possession of New Orleans fixes the sentence which is to restrain her forever within her low-water mark. It seals the union of two nations, who, in conjunction, can maintain exclusive possession of the ocean. From that moment, we must marry ourselves to the British fleet and nation. We must turn all our attention to a maritime force, for which our resources place us on very high ground; and, having formed and connected together a power which may render reinforcement of her settlements here impossible to France, make the first cannon which shall be fired in Europe the signal for tearing up any settlement she may have made, and for holding the two continents of America in sequestration for the common purposes of the united British and American nations.

Jefferson had been the great supporter of the more radically democratic view among our Founding Fathers. He had been an outstanding friend of France. But once the vital corporate interests of the United States were involved he was prepared to recommend that course of action which their defense seemed to require.

It was in the early decades of this century that our previously protected situation began to dissolve. The events of the years from 1914 through 1920 forced upon President Wilson the necessity of attempting to reconcile the protection of vital United States interests with a projection of our democratic principles to the world scene. It is with anguish that one follows the course of his endeavor and its failure on the stubborn rocks first of world politics and then of domestic politics.

Much has been written about the utopianism of Wilson's approach. In part these criticisms have validity. Wilson undoubtedly placed exaggerated hopes on the force of moral suasion and on the power of the opinions of mankind. The system which he envisaged could hardly have been expected to succeed unless all the great powers had shared a common political creed.   But to go to the opposite extreme, to stress only the promotion of narrow national interests, by whatever means seem at the moment expedient, would be to ignore entirely one of the great assets and hopes of our democratic tradition.

Since Wilson's time a second world war has been fought, the power position of nations has further changed, and there has been a further development of broad historical forces of tension and of contradiction.

A new generation has come to maturity.   It is only in a limited sense that traditions are passed on.   Each succeeding generation must largely rewin its own traditions in the real struggle of its own time.

And thus we come down to the present.   How, today, do the two broad streams which we have been discussing, the one springing from the stream of world history, the other springing from our own particular traditions and institutions, interact in the formulation of our foreign policy?

Let me repeat that the situation confronting the world and confronting the United States is this: That no combination of nations capable of standing up to the new threat represented by Soviet power is possible without active and permanent participation and leadership on the part of the United States.

By the same token the United States can no longer afford to take a passive attitude regarding its own security. This nation can no longer leave to other nations the task of preserving a world balance protective of our situation for it is beyond the capacity of others to do so.

The risks with which we are threatened are diverse and interrelated.   One risk is general, all-out war initiated by the U.S.S.R. either by direct attack on us or on one or more of our principle allies.   Another risk is localized communist military aggression.   Another is the loss of arms or positions important to the West through internal weakness, intimidation, or subversion.   Another is the risk of a general weakening and splitting up of the cohesiveness, will, and power of coordinated action of the free world coalition.   And finally there is the domestic risk of loss of fortitude, restraint, and faith in our own institutions.

No one of these risks can we afford to ignore.   There is a temptation to concentrate solely on the first and on the last: the risks of all-out war and the risks to our domestic institutions.

Carried to an extreme this temptation could lead us to the greatest dangers. We can emphasize the deterring of global war by atomic means to a point where we bring on our heads the very war we are trying to deter. We can emphasize the danger of internal subversion to a point where we undermine not only our capacity rationally to conduct our foreign affairs, but undermine our democratic processes as well.

But the particular danger which I wish to stress is the danger that we turn away from the responsibilities which have fallen to us with respect to the free world coalition.

It would seem to me that we can do so only if we are prepared gradually to withdraw under pressure to this hemisphere accepting the prospect of Asia, Europe, the Middle East, and possibly Africa, being gradually added to the enemy sphere. Then our survival, even as a secondary power, would become contingent on whether or not the Kremlin, unopposed by any power comparable to their own, could successfully coerce and organize the rest of the world. Cut off from the rest of mankind, subjected to mounting external pressures and humiliations, the time would not be long before domestic faction and dissension destroyed such of our internal freedoms as still remained. We would then have lost that external climate in which our democratic experiment can survive and prosper.

The other course, the course of responsible leadership of the free world coalition, is not easy. It requires that we take no narrow view. It means, above all else, that we must regard the vital interests of those peoples and nations who are members of the coalition as being associated with our own most basic interests. The purposes and policies we pursue must be broad enough to embrace the essential interest of the whole group. The essence of leadership is the successful resolution of problems and the successful attainment of objectives important to those whom one is called upon to lead.

To carry out a course of responsible leadership as a world power does require a modification in some of the conceptions which became firmly established during the long century in which ours was a protected situation.

We have come a long way in making these modifications in the last few years, particularly in the years from

1947 to 1952. That period saw the Truman doctrine and the associated program of aid to Greece and Turkey, the Marshall Plan, Point Four, the spread of our system of alliances to cover this hemisphere, most of Europe, and much of the Pacific, the military assistance programs bolstering the defensive capacity of our allies, the rebuilding of our own military establishment, the decision to proceed with the hydrogen bomb, the repulsion of aggression by collective action in Korea.

Perhaps, in the years 1947 to 1952, we moved in the direction of modifying and adapting our ideas and actions to our new position in the world at a rate faster than we could sustain. Perhaps a period of falling back in order to consolidate our position was necessary.

Perhaps the national debates on the Bricker Amendment,[*] on the so-called new look in our defense policy, on McCarthyism and on Indo-China were necessary.

But in the longer run—and we may not have much time—the process of bringing our concepts and actions in the field of foreign policy into closer relation with the facts of the external world must continue.

This does not require a change in the beliefs informing our American traditions. In fact it is our belief in truth, in the dignity of the common man, in the consent of the governed, in the independence of nations, in a decent respect to the opinions of mankind, which is the core of our psychological strength and the force which, if backed by adequate material strength, can attract to our leadership nations and peoples all over the world.

---

[*] *A proposed amendment to the Constitution, sponsored by Republican Senator John W. Bricker of Ohio, to give Congress the power to veto any executive agreement and place restrictions on the president's treaty-making authority. The amendment died in the Senate in February 1954.*

12. The Effect of New Weapons
Systems on Our Alliances*

(1957)

I

As one looks back over the course of history, the politics of alliances and coalitions does not appear to be particularly sensitive to developments in weapons technology.

---

*In "The Effect of New Weapons Systems On Our Alliances," a pamphlet derived from a speech he made to the Council on Foreign Relations in 1957, Nitze examined the growing interaction between alliance politics and modern military technology. Though it seemed to encompass the entire range of armaments, the term "new weapons," as used in the 1950s, was actually a euphemism that the Eisenhower administration often substituted when it meant nuclear weapons, especially the so-called "tactical" variety. Accepting this usage, Nitze argued that new weapons had done little to enhance NATO's security because the Soviets had shown themselves capable of deploying similar new weapons of their own, thereby nullifying whatever advantage the West may have felt it achieved. Short of all-out nuclear retaliation, Nitze added, NATO was virtually defenseless since alliance strategy and weaponry provided for no credible defense by non-nuclear means. Nitze arranged for his speech to be privately printed in limited quantity, but by word of mouth it soon attracted considerable attention and Nitze was inundated with requests for copies, including a request from the NATO Supreme Commander, General Lauris Norstad.

One can read Thucydides or Polybius with the impression that much of what they had to say about alliances and their politics remains fully relevant today. In so far as one can piece together the politics of that period of Chinese history known as the period of the Warring States analogous problems arose and found analogous answers. Similarly one can study the interstate politics of Florence or Milan or Venice during the Renaissance or the politics of the period of nation states in Europe from the Peace of Westphalia to the first World War and the pattern of shifting alliances, the struggle to maintain a balance of power, the tendency for coalitions to form in opposition to the strongest power, the interplay between internal class tensions, and external power politics display similar characteristics.

During this span of history there were great and far-reaching developments in military technology. Obviously the developments of improved steel, improved armor, fortifications, the cross-bow, fire arms, artillery, and the machine guns as well as improvements in strategy and tactics and in the organization of large armies, all had an important influence on what statesmen did and on how the crucial battles were decided. But the fact that one can read Thucydides today with such a feeling that the problems he discusses are our problems, raises a question as to the degree to which the politics of alliances are dependent upon military technology or merely form the ever changing background against which the ageless game of politics is played.

II

The very formulation of our topic implies a certain approach to the problem. Our topic is the "Impact of Modern Weapons Systems Upon Our Alliances." One can conceive of different formulations which would carry quite other implications. For instance, the question could have been phrased, "What weapons systems should we develop and concentrate on, to support the political objectives of our alliance system most effectively?" The first formulation suggests a cause and effect relationship running from modern military technology to alliances. The second formulation suggests that the political purpose comes first and that the choice of appropriate weapons systems, within the possibilities of modern scientific technology, comes second as a means toward an end.

Perhaps one can state the problem most succinctly by asking the question whether our alliance system today is a means to increase the effectiveness with which modern weapons systems can be brought to contribute to our security, or whether appropriate weapons systems are the means we select to contribute to the basic interests of our allies as well as of ourselves. In the main I believe the second proposition rather than the first deserves our support.

Clausewitz discusses a closely related point when he deals with the relationship of military strategy to political policy. He takes strong exception to those who argue that political policy should be subordinated to the requirements of military strategy. He grants that political policy must take into account the possibilities and requirements of military strategy. His point is that political policy must take into account not only military considerations, but many other considerations as well, and that military strategy not subordinated to political policy becomes a dangerous and a senseless thing.

But how does all this apply to our problems today? Today we are under threat of attack by an immense and hostile power possessing thermonuclear weapons and the means of delivery which, if not now capable of destroying us, will in all probability reach this capability in the next few years. Is this not the prime fact of our existence today and do not all other facts have to take a subordinate position to this one? Obviously the answer is "no." If it were "yes," all we would have to do is elect Mr. Khrushchev or his nominee president of the United States and there would be no reason for Russia to threaten us with thermonuclear weapons at all. She could exercise complete control through less offensive means. We *do* put peace with justice ahead of mere survival. We have no intention of giving up our political souls just because the Russians have thermonuclear weapons. The Russians, the British, the Indians, the Turks, and even the Egyptians feel similarly. They have not in the past, and do not in the future propose to surrender their political ideas or objectives just because we have had in the past, and we, the Russians, and the British have now, the physical means to incinerate them.

III

As one looks back over the changes which the last fifty years brought about from the political system which prevailed in the preceding century it seems to me that the nature of the political problem which we as a nation face in the world emerges more clearly.

During the long century from 1815 to the first World War the principal fact of international politics was the Concert of Europe. The European powers felt a responsibility for what went on in the world, for preventing any one power from achieving a universal hegemony, for limiting the incidence of war and the objectives for which wars were fought, and for preserving a political and economic climate in which a measure of development, not only for themselves but others was possible. Britain was the key figure politically, militarily, and economically in maintaining that system and we, the United States, and to some extent Japan, were the principal beneficiaries.

The two world wars have destroyed not only the system but the empires which composed it. The Austro-Hungarian Empire and the Ottoman Empire no longer exist even in name. The British, the French, the German, and the Italian empires either no longer exist or are too weakened to carry a leading world role. Japan was defeated and shorn of its gains. And the Russian Empire was destroyed and control of its land, its people, and its great resources captured by a regime with an alien and hostile philosophy. During a fifty-year span the forest of great powers has been felled and two giant trees are left standing one of which is of a strange and exotic breed.

I have heard one of our wisest diplomats predict that when the history of this century is written it will show that the central fact of this period was not the rise of the Soviet Union but the decline of England. I think that what he was getting at was that from the standpoint of United States foreign policy the outstanding development was not that the U.S.S.R. arose as a hostile power threatening us. There have always been great and threatening powers in the world. It was rather that the system of world order which England had done so much, particularly during the nineteenth century, to maintain had broken down and that it fell to the lot of the United States to attempt to construct in its place some new system of order.

The Soviet leaders are obviously throwing every road block they can in the way of our succeeding in constructing such a system. It therefore looks from time to time as though there were only one main political fact of these times, namely, Russian hostility. I would suggest that equally important political facts are the crying need for some system of international order and the fact that no one but the United States is in a position to give leadership and strength to the building of such a system.

IV

The current situation differs from that of the nine-teenth century in many ways. From the point of view of this discussion the most important is probably the disproportion in power between the two greatest powers and the others. In the middle of the twentieth century we find ourselves in a period of two coalitions, the Western world, dependent for leadership on the United States, and the Sino-Soviet system.

The first is held together only by consent growing out of self-interest and the second in part by coercion—the European satellites—and in part by consent—China.

In spite of the very great relative strength of the United States and of the U.S.S.R. neither is by itself either in a position to defeat the other or to create and maintain a world system satisfactory to its interests and its concepts of justice. Each therefore requires the support of the other members of its coalition. In fact the balance of political power between the two systems is so close that any substantial movement of the states in one coalition to the other would probably be decisive in giving to the latter the margin of strength and prestige necessary to establish a general system of order conforming to its conceptions.

The heart of the international political struggle is therefore the battle between coalitions which is now going on. History gives us very clear rules for coalition warfare.

The first rule is: Whatever increases the strength or coherence of one's own group, or decreases the strength or coherence of the other is good.

The second rule is: Whatever does the opposite is bad.

The third rule is: If the same act can both strengthen your group and weaken the other this is best of all.

So our purpose as leaders of the Western coalition is twofold. On the one hand to check, weaken, balance, and contain the Sino-Soviet coalition and, if driven to it, to prevail over it. On the other hand it is to create a workable non-Soviet world, in which diversity can flourish and which will be sufficiently effective in meeting the various demands of members of the group to build wide tolerance for the system and, if possible, the loyalty to make it stable.

The test of leadership is whether one makes reasonable progress in promoting the basic interests of those one is attempting to lead. They must be convinced that their interests are better off with your leadership than without it. Does it really produce results for the led and not just for the leader? Is its policy addressed to the fundamental issues, fundamental not just today but in the long run?

V

So far I have been talking fairly loosely about the coalition which looks to us for leadership. Historically the great coalitions have had their origin in a definite and obvious threat from some one power to achieve hegemony over the entire group. Some foundation of common conceptions and similar approaches to fundamental political questions was generally a prerequisite. But the catalyst which caused the coalition to coalesce was always the clear and overt threat presented by either a state within the system, or some outside state, attempting to achieve a general dominion. Today the threat is from the Soviet Union. Let us hope that it never appears to come from us because if it did we could be certain that a grand coalition in opposition to us would arise.

The coalition today can be viewed as including all those countries who propose to seek their political future along some line other than under Soviet control or hegemony and are prepared to resist any encroachment on that independent line of development. Certainly Sweden, Switzerland, Austria, and Finland, in this sense are members of the coalition. Probably Yugoslavia and perhaps even Poland should be included. India and Burma should definitely be included. None of these countries are members of our alliance system, unless one includes responsible membership in the United Nations and dedication to its principles as qualifying a country to be considered an ally. We did go to the armed support of the Republic of Korea even though we were under no treaty obligation, apart from our commitments under the United Nations, to go to her support. Almost all the other non-communist countries of the world cannot only be included within the coalition, as I have used the term, but are also tied to us and we to them by specific treaty commitment. The point could be made that we are not a signatory to the Baghdad Pact, but we are a member of its military committee and under the Eisenhower doctrine have taken full commitment to its support.

We consider that an important element of the threat presented by the Sino-Soviet block is the military threat and that it requires joint planning, organization, and preparation to provide the coordinated forces and facilities which will give the necessary hope and assurance that the Soviet military threat can be resisted, and if necessary, overcome. But not all members of the coalition share that view.

The Indian, the Pakistani, the Burmese, and even the Japanese people see little danger of direct military aggression against themselves in the immediate future. The government leaders in those countries would be faced with very great internal problems if they were to make very substantial sacrifices of what their people consider to be their national interests in order to support a greater common riposte to the threat of Sino-Soviet military aggression. The very words "treaty" and "alliance" are to Asians Western words with connotations of capitulations, extraterritoriality, and colonialism.

It is therefore impossible to build an alliance system which is coterminous with the coalition. Alliances can serve a variety of functions. They can define a mutuality of strategic interests. They can serve notice to hostile powers that encroachment beyond a certain point will elicit a common response. They can provide a legal foundation for planning and for action. Alliances can provide a symbol around which a pre-existing or developing consensus can be organized and strengthened.

To be effective alliances should be built upon a fundamental community of interests and a common harmonious overall strategic concept.

If they are really to serve notice against encroachment, or constitute a legal basis for longer-term planning or action, or provide a symbol of real political force they should not be subject to drastic amendment if there is a normal overturn in the domestic political leadership within one or more of the member countries, and they should not be based upon ephemeral or misunderstood considerations.

VI

As one surveys the alliance system of which we are the central link, NATO, O.A.S., SEATO, ANZUS, the Baghdad Pact and the bilateral treaties with the Chinese Nationalists on Formosa, with the Republic of Korea, and with Japan, what general impression does one get? To me it is hardly reassuring.

Originally NATO most nearly filled all the criteria of a strong alliance. Its principal countries have a great community of political interest. A common strategic doctrine was developed and constituted a basis for common planning and action which otherwise would have been impossible. The purposes of NATO were well understood not only by the member governments but by the mass of informed citizens. And most important of all NATO has been a symbol of the furthest and deepest commitment of power of North America to the support of Europe.

ANZUS and O.A.S, though less solidly based in a community of interests and a common strategic concept, were supported by geographic considerations and were not called upon to carry the same political burden as was NATO. The other arrangements were always more weakly based and subject to obvious strains.

Today even NATO shows major strains. In part these strains can be attributed to the disaster of Suez and to the effort of the Soviets to relax tensions and by emphasizing the policy of co-existence to reduce the fear of Soviet hegemony which originally called the coalition and the alliance system into being.

I would suggest that there is a deeper and more underlying factor that is undermining our alliance structure. This factor is the developing pattern of modern weapons systems, the strategic posture we have taken with respect to those systems, and the statements we have made about that strategy.

The very existence of weapons systems such as those either in actual existence today or on the immediate technological horizon create a problem for the survival of our alliance system. England is faced today with the prospect that six thermonuclear bombs of large size would blanket the British Isles with either blast or highly radioactive fall-out. The prospect of defense against planes carrying such weapons with the short distances available for radar tracking is formidable. The prospect of countering the intermediate range rockets which the Russians have been testing in large numbers is almost inconceivable. For none of our other allies, except possibly Canada and Australia, is the position much better.

Until recently most of our allies have felt that even though they were relatively defenseless against nuclear attack from the U.S.S.R., we were not and that in being allied with us they shared in the security which the combination of our geographic position and our strong strategic capabilities provided to the system as a whole. They have felt that alliance with us protected them not only against nuclear attack from the U.S.S.R. but that our superior nuclear atomic capabilities provided a shield against other, non-nuclear, forms of Sino-Soviet military aggression as well.

With the prospective development of Russian delivery means capable of devastating the United States this prospect becomes less certain. We have all read the newspaper reports of testimony before the Congress that 250 ten megaton weapons dropped in the continental United States could be expected to result in casualties of some eighty odd million killed and forty odd million injured provided there were no warning, no evacuation of our cities, and no prepared shelters. We are not doing anything to provide shelters or organize evacuation. With a growing Soviet fleet of long-range jet bombers and refueling techniques 250 weapons dropped within the continental limits does not seem to be an inconceivable number. With the development of intercontinental missiles or submarine-based intermediate range missiles the problems of defense become even more difficult.

To fight a nuclear war makes no sense for either of the possible major participants or for any of its allied or associated countries unless the initial phase of the war is completely one-sided and decisive and is fought almost entirely on somebody else's territory. While we had a monopoly of atomic weapons this was a possibility. Today any such possibility is extremely dim unless the attacking side attacks with consummate deception and surprise and the attacked side is delinquent in taking the obvious but expensive precautions of dispersal, hardened bases, adequate warning systems, and continuous ready alert.

The function of preparation for nuclear war is then primarily to provide a deterrent. A deterrent to be effective must be a threat which is believed. It will be believed only if both the capacity and the intention to use that capacity are reasonably evident. The intention to use a capacity will hardly be believed unless the issue bears some reasonable relations to the force which that issue is to evoke.

The reason NATO is not in deeper trouble than it is today is that from the standpoint of the European powers the presence of five and a half United States divisions in Germany makes it highly probable that any Soviet attack on Europe would call S.A.C. into action. Rather than face a humiliating defeat of a major force of that size the United States could be expected to loose its strategic air arm no matter what destruction we could expect would be visited upon our cities in retaliation. From the standpoint of the Germans, the French, and the British it is the five and a half United States divisions, backed by S.A.C. which constitute the deterrent. The British, French, and German divisions make little actual contribution to the deterrent. Under current strategic concepts it is understandable why the Europeans are reluctant to raise additional divisions or even maintain those now under arms. They do not really make a strategic contribution. They are necessary politically in order to provide a facade of common forces without which we might be tempted to withdraw ours.

It seems to me quite understandable that many intelligent Europeans doubt the long-range stability of the present arrangements. I have a hard time seeing the United States maintain sizable forces in Europe indefinitely merely for the purpose of providing a trip-wire which, while all goes well, may provide a deterrent for the defense of Europe but which, if something went wrong, could involve us in universal destruction at home.

I believe we can and should maintain our divisions in Europe for a reasonable period in the future until we have had time to work out an alternative solution and this may unavoidably be a period of a decade or more. But to look upon it as a permanent solution fills me with misgivings.

The Russians obviously consider the presence of United States forces in Europe to be on the one hand the greatest obstacle to the success of their own policies and on the other a point of vulnerability in our political positions. It is against these troops that the full force of Soviet policy is today turned.

VII

What alternative solutions can one look forward to in the future?

One would be a negotiation with the Russians under which they withdrew behind the Bug and we withdrew from Germany or from the continent. If this resulted in a reunification of Germany and the liberation of the Eastern satellites it would have much to recommend it. We would, however, have to give the closest attention to measures which would continue to provide the necessary deterrent. Perhaps greater German, British, and French air and ground strength, perhaps intercontinental missiles, perhaps submarine-based missiles, would provide the capacity. The problem would be to make sure that the Russians are convinced of our intention really to engage forces adequate to enable the Europeans fully to counter whatever the Russians might throw in. To provide proof of intention as persuasive as the presence of United States troops is not easy.

An equally serious point is that the prospect for any sound negotiation with the Russians is poor unless we have an alternative that we are prepared to live with for the long run, in the event the Russians take a recalcitrant position on any essential point during the negotiation. We are bound to be forced into an improvident deal with the Russians if we are in a position where we have to have their agreement, where we have no clear alternative which is about as good for us and worse for the Russians than the deal we are trying to make.

We must therefore continue to concern ourselves with the question of what it is we and NATO should do in the absence of an agreement with the Soviets.

Should we put greater reliance upon tactical atomic weapons? Should we supply our allies with such weapons? Should we encourage them to develop long-range strategic nuclear weapons systems of their own? Should we advocate a great effort to build up non-nuclear forces which could provide a reasonable defense against non-nuclear attack and permit us to restrict the nuclear deterrent solely to the role of deterring nuclear attack?

The latter policy is the alternative which I would back. This would be tantamount to reversing the massive retaliation doctrine which Mr. Dulles announced before this Council in the spring of 1954. Instead of increasing our reliance upon nuclear weapons to support our alliance system and our foreign policy in general, we would attempt to reduce that reliance. The cost of implementing such a policy would be great. We could expect no great savings in providing the nuclear deterrent against nuclear attack. The building of adequate conventional forces would be expensive in men and in money. But the political gains would be immense in having strategic doctrine which makes sense for the long run, which we can explain to our allies, and which will give their contribution to the strategy of the alliance a real and not just a psychological importance.

VIII

During the closing months of World War II and the initial post-war period the United States Strategic Bombing Survey conducted an elaborate study which attempted to assess some of the strategic lessons that were to be learned from our World War II experience both in Europe and in the Pacific. As we looked into the future one of the points that worried us was the probable political reaction to American forces stationed abroad as the years stretched out into the indefinite future. Occupation forces have almost invariably inspired hatred. Even allied forces have caused friction whenever the strategic justification, in the interest of the country in which they are stationed, is not clear.

As I said earlier the strategic justification of our forces in Europe, in providing the proof of our intent, is an essential element to the deterrent strategy which is the only strategy we and our allies in NATO now have.

In the Far East the military threat that our allies see is the threat from Communist China. The Chinese Communists are not believed to have atomic weapons. The power of the United States must therefore shield them, not against nuclear attack the threat of which they do not take seriously, but against Chinese Communist attack with conventional weapons. But even the military threat from China looks less and less real to them as the years pass on after the Korean intervention. In Formosa and Japan we see the underlying strains which are bound to exist in the long-term stationing of troops with differing standards, customs, and concepts of justice. Both the threat which necessitates the presence of foreign troops and the strategy which we have in mind to meet that threat must be manifestly clear and understandable if trouble is to be avoided.

The more we talk about the threat from enemy thermonuclear weapons and our primary strategic reliance upon super-weapons of our own the less persuasive do the requirements for the Pacific and Southeast Asian parts of our alliance system seem to our partners. What is the use of thirty ground division on Formosa if in any case B-52s from bases in the United States are going to devastate mainland China in the event Formosa is attacked? The justification of our strategy will become even more difficult if it ever appears that the Chinese have nuclear weapons of their own or have been given them by the Russians.

IX

In conclusion let me summarize.

The political problem of the United States is not just that of countering a military threat from the U.S.S.R. but is that of creating a world system with some degree of hope and stability to take the place of the one that was shattered by the two world wars. The coalition of the free world and its supporting alliance system must contribute not just to our security requirements but to the basic interests of the coalition as a whole. There are great difficulties in maintaining in the long run a strategy which depends almost entirely on the deterrent effect of super-weapons. In my view super-weapons should in the long run be relied upon only to assure that they will not be used by others. We therefore face the urgent necessity of developing a strategy which will apply to all the other manifold military problems which can arise in the building of a more acceptable world order.

"The Effect of New Weapons Systems on Our Alliances" was originally printed by Overbrook Press (Stamford, Conn.: 1957), the personal press of the late Frank Altschul.

13. Alternatives to NATO*

(1959)

In discussing alternatives to NATO, there are several possible approaches to our subject.

One approach is focus on prediction. We can look at the present status of NATO in comparison with its status at various times in the past. We can analyze the forces which appear to be behind the trends of change that have taken place. We can then attempt to extrapolate those forces and trends forward in time and arrive at an estimate of the new situation we will probably face at some time in the future.

In January 1959 Nitze appeared at Princeton University as a speaker to a conference on NATO strategy. Later that same year the organizer of the conference, Klaus Knorr, included a slightly revised version of Nitze's remarks in a compilation of conference papers that is still widely used and read today. Nitze's contribution was typical of his style and method of analysis. It evaluates the political and military problems NATO was likely to face in the future, reviews the full spectrum of courses of action the alliance might take to respond, and draws from this analysis common sense conclusions. In assessing what he termed "alternatives to NATO," Nitze put little weight on either a U.S. withdrawal to a "Fortress America" concept, or on the possibility that one or several European countries might adopt a neutralist stance. However, he did warn that American prestige and leadership within the alliance were eroding and correctly predicted that some countries—France in particular—would increasingly adopt independent policies that could threaten NATO unity.

This should give us an insight into the various alternatives to, or major modifications of, NATO which would seem possible in that new situation.

A second approach is to concentrate on a functional analysis. What today are the major elements of NATO and what are their functions? How could those elements and functions be modified or changed over the spectrum of conceivable alternatives?

A third approach is to examine, not what is likely to happen, nor what conceivably could happen, but what we should be trying to make happen in the interest of overall policy.

These three approaches are not mutually exclusive. In fact, they are complementary. An extrapolation forward of current trends gives one a sense of the real problems which must be faced and of the limits of the solutions that are within the realm of the practically possible. A survey of the major elements of NATO, of their functions, and of the full spectrum of conceivable alternatives helps to point up possibilities which might otherwise be overlooked. Finally, a discussion of probable trends and conceivable alternatives would be meaningless unless we eventually came to grips with the policy question: In what direction should the will and effort of the United States be directed to mold the future rather than merely to adapt to it?

Before getting into the substance of these three approaches, it may be useful to define a little more precisely what we mean by an alternative to NATO. In addition to new systems which would involve the elimination of NATO or its supersession by a new organization, changes in NATO so substantial as to exceed a mere modification or development of the alliance are considered to be alternatives to it. These could include such radical changes as the elimination from the membership of NATO of one or more of its principal members—the United States, the United Kingdom, France, or Germany—or the addition of sufficient non-Atlantic members to destroy its present regional character. They could include changes in its organizational structure that would strengthen its cohesion so radically as to make NATO a confederation, or that would weaken it so radically as to reduce it to a mere political commitment. Furthermore, it is possible to conceive of changes in the philosophy underlying NATO so radical as to constitute an alternative, even though no change were made in its membership or in the form of its organization. Today it is assumed that a collective defense of the NATO countries is possible and that, in the long run, the U.S.S.R. can be made to accept and live with that fact. If the reverse assumption were to be accepted, the purpose of NATO would logically become that of finding the best accommodation possible with the U.S.S.R. Such a change in the basic assumption underlying the purpose of NATO would constitute as radical an alternative as any of the others suggested.

I

Let me now turn to the trends of the past, the principal forces that seem to have been behind those trends, and their extrapolation into the future. These trends can only be suggested in a most tentative way. The period of history with which we are dealing is too close to us for a more precise judgment.

The following trends come to mind: The first is a trend from political commitment to collective defense and then back toward re-emphasis upon political commitment rather than collective defense. NATO began as a treaty registering mutual commitments of its members. The relevant commitment was that of the United States to come to the support of Western Europe should it be attacked. Very quickly this basically political commitment was transformed into the beginning of a collective defense posture. With the commitment of American, British, and Canadian divisions to Europe under an American supreme commander, this trend took a major forward stride. It continued until the force goals set by the Lisbon Conference failed of implementation.* Since that time, there has been a steady weakening of the collective defense posture of NATO relative to that of the Soviet Union. The corollary has been greater reliance upon the political commitment, backed by the deterrence provided by SAC.

At its meeting in Lisbon in February 1952, the North Atlantic Council agreed that NATO should strive for 50 ready divisions by the end of the year for the defense of Western Europe. This strength was never attained.

A second trend has been that affecting the role of the United States within NATO. Originally the pressure was from the European members, who sought greater United States initiative and leadership. For a period that leadership was willingly provided by the United States and was cooperatively accepted by the European members. There followed a period of more hesitant leadership by the United States and even that leadership was accepted with increasing reluctance. The culmination of this trend found its expression in the Suez crisis. There has been some recovery since, but American leadership, either in its provision or in its acceptance, is today not to be taken for granted.

A third trend was, in first, increasing NATO pressure against the Central European satellites of Russia, followed, since the suppression of the Hungarian uprising, by increasing Soviet bloc pressure against Europe.

Now, what have been the forces which have underlain these trends?

One force has been a decrease in the incremental advantages which Europe could expect to receive from the United States connection. As European economic recovery has progressed, economic assistance has come to be of marginal rather than of fundamental importance to the principal European countries. With the full commitment of such United States military forces to the Continent as it appears reasonable to anticipate, additions to NATO non-nuclear military strength must of necessity come largely from the European countries themselves. Another factor in Europe's decreased expectations has been the greater emphasis in United States policy on United States interests rather than on the collective interests of the NATO members considered as a group. This has caused them to expect less United States support for European interests in non-NATO areas such as the Middle East and South Asia.

A second force has been the fundamental change in nuclear power relationships. The most important components of this force have been the growth in Soviet nuclear stockpiles, the lead the Soviets seem to have established in long-range missile technology, and the impressive indications of relative Soviet progress in basic research and rate of economic expansion. Another component has been the progressive nuclearization of war planning and preparation on the Western side, and increasing public knowledge in the

West as to the probable effects of such a war on civilians. This second force has tended to offset the strength of the deterrence which the United States connection could be expected to provide and to increase the risks to the European countries implied by that connection.

A third force is to be found in the shifting power relations and political strains within NATO. One component in this force has been the growing power and political stature, first, of Germany, and now possibly of France, vis-a-vis England. In the early days of NATO, the combined influence of the United States and England could usually bring unity into NATO policy decisions. Today that is no longer true. Another component has been the divisive effect of such issues as Cyprus, Algiers, the China policy of the United States, the free-trade area, and Icelandic fishing. On the other side of this equation, one should, however, mention the diminishing distrust and growing rapport between France and Germany. The growth in stature of the Community of Six, adding the Common Market and Euratom to the Coal and Steel Community, provides the prospect both of increased strength and cohesion on the Continent and of difficult problems to be worked out between the Community of Six and the other NATO and OEEC members.

A NATO structure which has shown these trends and which has been affected by these forces is now to be tested by a concerted Soviet pressure drive. At present this drive is centered on the exposed position of Berlin and the desire of the German people for reunification, a reunification which can take place only with Russian consent. The context of this drive is a weakened NATO relationship. The Soviet objective is the elimination of United States forces and influence from Berlin, from Germany, and from Europe.

It is in the light of this impending test of NATO that we must examine conceivable alternatives.

II

Now, what are the principal elements of NATO and their functions, and are there alternative methods of satisfying these functions?

We can list five elements. The first is the drawing of a line which will give the Soviet bloc clear notice of the American commitment to intervene should the line be violated. The second is the presence of sufficient American forces in Europe to make it clear that we intend to honor the commitment. The third is the provision of sufficient collective forces to restrain a substantial probing attack—a military attack short of a major invasion of Western Europe. The fourth is the provision of ready and secure forces properly positioned to deter a major Soviet attack. The fifth is an organizational framework and political symbol around which the principal Western powers can coordinate their political, economic, and general power so as to create a power center adequate to balance the coordinated general power of the Communist bloc.

Now, the drawing of a line which will define a United States commitment to intervene, should it be violated, can be done in several ways. It can be done by unilateral declaration by the president. It can be done by joint resolution of the Congress. It can be conveyed to Moscow through diplomatic channels as a specific and concrete warning. The question is whether the Soviet leaders will believe that we really mean it; that in the face of the overwhelming military and very great political power which they can mobilize against a particular position, we and our allies will, in fact, take serious and effective action if the line we draw is breached.

One of the factors which tends to make a commitment credible is the formality and authority of the procedure by which it was originally registered. The most formal and authoritative commitment the United States can make is obviously a treaty commitment. The requirement of approval by two-thirds of the Senate ensures that the decision to enter into the commitment is not one of individuals, or of a single party, but is a solid expression of national will and intent. A loss of national honor would be involved if the United States were to back down on a treaty commitment under pressure. Bilateral treaty commitments covering Western Europe would not be as logical a solution to the problem of drawing a line as the present NATO multilateral treaty. It is doubtful whether the Senate would be likely to accept them as an alternative unless the most compelling considerations were advanced. In summary, there are other ways of drawing a line, but these other ways are less credible and serious than the present NATO commitment.

Regarding the second element we have listed—the presence of sufficient United States forces in Europe to make it clear that our commitment is backed by a serious intention—we are again concerned with convincing the U.S.S.R. that we really will act if the NATO line is breached. Today Russian forces could not overrun the Continent without overrunning the five and one-half United States divisions stationed there. It is hardly conceivable that we could permit those divisions to be overwhelmed without bringing to bear against the U.S.S.R. the full force of every weapon we possess. The presence of these forces in effect transfers the weight of Russian pressure from Western Europe to the SAC bases in the United States. Is there any alternative means by which a similar deterrent to Soviet military pressure against Europe can be provided? Perhaps a smaller number of American divisions, reinforced from time to time in periods of crisis, might have substantially the same effect. It is difficult, however, to conceive either how these forces can be kept indefinitely in Europe except under the legitimization of their presence provided by NATO, or how any deterrent of equal persuasiveness could be substituted if they were to be removed.

The third element which we have listed is the provision of sufficient collective forces to make it possible to restrain a substantial probing attack—a military attack short of all-out war. American forces permanently stationed on the Continent should not, in the long run, be essential to the performance of this function. An adequate number of German, French, and Italian divisions properly equipped should be able to do so. The presence of United States and British forces does, however, tend to stiffen the line. In any case, some form of collective defense understanding would seem to be required if any of the Western European countries is to stand up to and throw back a probing attack of any considerable strength. To stand up alone against even a two-or three-division attack which includes Soviet forces is more than can be expected of any of the Western European powers.

The fourth element is the provision of ready and secure forces properly positioned to deter a major Soviet attack. This element has three components. The first is the provision of shield forces on the Continent. As pointed out earlier, these forces have been permitted since Lisbon to decline in relative strength. The second is the provision of tactical nuclear forces to back up the shield. Against larger Soviet forces similarly equipped, they contribute largely by knitting together the deterrence of the shield with that of the sword. The credibility of the sword itself, however, is now subject to question, except as against the most extreme provocation. It is not always recognized that there is an inverse relationship between the strength of the sword and the degree of provocation which it can be expected to deter. With the advent of Soviet ICBMs, a successful counterforce strike by SAC (even in riposte to an attack on Europe and thus with benefit of the first nuclear strike) becomes hardly credible. It therefore becomes of the utmost importance to all members of the alliance that the contribution of the shield to deterrence be increased and that the power of the sword, relative to Soviet forces, not be permitted to decline further.

The relevance of NATO to the shield forces is obvious. A question, however, can be raised as to the longer-term importance of the contribution which the NATO countries, other than the United States, can make to the sword. The importance of NATO in this regard is less clear than it once was. Today, a number of alternative solutions are conceivable for the future. The most obvious is reliance upon the Polaris submarine system at the periphery and the Minuteman system at the center. However, in a world in which nuclear weapons are each capable of destruction over a large area, sheer geographic extent and diversity of defense and retaliatory means become important factors. It is by no means clear that reliance upon any one or two weapon systems can give such certainty of retaliation as to provide a sufficiently credible deterrent. Until these phases have been completed and the actual systems are in place, geographic diversity of retaliatory means is of the utmost importance. Western Europe alone, or the United States alone, does not provide an adequate base for a credible deterrent against a provocation short of an all-out nuclear attack. Each is therefore dependent upon the other. Without NATO the means of satisfying this interdependence for defense are difficult to imagine.

The fifth element we have listed is the organizational framework and political symbol provided by NATO as a center around which the Western powers can coordinate their political, economic, and general power so as to create a power center adequate to balance the coordinated general power of the Communist bloc.

It can be argued that NATO provides only a weak organizational framework; that as a political symbol it is somewhat tarnished by its necessary concentration on military defense; that as a power center it is too exclusive and alienates rather than attracts those nations in the Middle East, Asia, and Africa where the general power of the Communist bloc presents its greatest challenge; and that more important than a regional organization and a regional political symbol are the strength, wise policy, and unity of the individual nations. There is some substance to these arguments. The fact remains, however, that strength, wisdom of policy, and unity among nations do not come about easily or automatically. NATO has played an important role in bringing the North Atlantic powers closer together than they would have been without it. If NATO were to be done away with today and nothing substituted in its place, it is quite possible that the centrifugal forces always present even between nations whose basic interests are close together might well become dominant. It is quite conceivable that the major continental Western European nations, in the absence of NATO, would put their primary reliance on the Community of Six and hope that a third-force position—a position of neutralism—would carry them through the international storms to be anticipated.

Before discussing further the full range of possible political alternatives to NATO, let us turn to the third of our methodological approaches, the approach from the standpoint of policy.

III

The principal policy issue affecting NATO today concerns two potentially conflicting objectives. One objective is to increase the power and firmness of the West in standing up to the adverse power of the Communist bloc. The other objective is to surmount the adversary relationship between East and West and work out some system of relationships between them which is more satisfactory and less hazardous than the present bleak confrontation.

These two objectives are not necessarily in conflict with each other. It can be argued that the greater the relative strength of the West to that of the East, the less have been the tensions between the two sides.   After the rapid build-up of strength in the West occasioned by the Korean War, and during the uncertain political relationships and readjustments in the East following Stalin's death, we saw the first Geneva Conference and the "spirit of Geneva." This is undoubtedly an oversimplified analysis. Many other developments were concurrently taking place.   These included the shift in Soviet doctrine from the concept of capitalist encirclement to that of two camps, coexistence, and the prospect of socialist encirclement of capitalism. Nevertheless, with the decline in relative Western strength and cohesiveness since the first Geneva Conference, we have seen an increase in tension which culminated, in 1958, in the virtual ultimatum concerning Berlin.

There are, however, legitimate grounds for deep anxiety concerning the long-range continuation of the present bleak confrontation, and therefore grounds for the consequent effort to find some alternate road.   There is growing public realization of the hazards involved in a potentially unstable nuclear "stalemate" in which great advantages may accrue to the side striking the initial blow. There are risks that, even with an extensive and protracted effort by the West to balance the power of the East, positions of importance to the West will be eroded and lost. Under the circumstances, much of Western public opinion demands that some more direct solution to these growing hazards be found through a negotiated settlement or partial settlement.   A wide variety of proposals have been put forward. Some of them imply the elimination of NATO, or at least some alternative of it.

The proposal most seriously debated is that an area in Central Europe be made into a buffer zone between East and West—that there be a disengagement between the military forces of the United States and the U.S.S.R. from their direct confrontation in the heart of Europe.

The degree of disengagement proposed has covered a wide spectrum. The more modest proposals call merely for a ban on nuclear weapons within some defined area or a general thinning of military forces on both sides within such an area. The intent, however, is that these modest steps be but the initial steps in a process which will then proceed to a more complete disengagement. The more radical proposals call for the prompt reunification of Germany, the with-drawal of Germany from NATO, the withdrawal of all United

States forces from Europe, and the withdrawal of Russian forces behind the Bug River, back behind the boundaries of the U.S.S.R.

A series of issues immediately arise in considering these proposals. One issue is the degree to which the proposed concessions and withdrawals on both sides are reasonably symmetrical and equitable in their effect. In 1948, some of us in the State Department were of the view that an agreement which achieved the substantial withdrawal of Russian forces behind the Bug River would be so highly beneficial in its effects, even if the United States forces were symmetrically withdrawn from Europe, that the West should strongly press for such an agreement. The most compelling reason against making such a proposal was that there seemed to be no possibility whatever that the Russians would agree to it. That they would not was fully confirmed during the meeting of the Council of Foreign Ministers at the Palais Rose in Paris in 1949. This experience emphasizes the second issue—the question of whether any given proposal will in fact be negotiable.

But let us go back, for a moment, and go a little more fully into the situation as it existed in 1948 and 1949. Those in the Policy Planning Staff who favored disengagement at that time were of the view that if Russian forces were withdrawn behind the Bug, a very substantial political reorientation was certain to take place in all of Central Europe. It was our hope that this reorientation would take place gradually and with discretion. We did not see how the reunification of Germany in a form acceptable to the Bonn government could be prevented if Russian military forces were not directly present in support of the East German regime. Far from wishing Germany or any other part of Central Europe to become part of NATO, it was our thought that the influence of the NATO powers would be directed to keeping Central Europe a buffer area incapable of disturbing the security of the West or of challenging the East. The United States monopoly of atomic weapons was considered a sufficient strategic guarantee to ensure that the U.S.S.R. did not violate the agreement.

Today the correlation of forces is quite different from what it was in 1948 and 1949. There is no longer an American atomic monopoly to guarantee any such agreement as might be made. But, more importantly, it is now the Russians who can hope that the effects of even a superficially symmetrical agreement will lead to the eventual withdrawal of American influence from Europe as a whole rather than to a withdrawal of Russian influence from Central Europe. Respect for the brute power of the U.S.S.R., and for its will to use superior strength to prevent forces antagonistic to the Soviet Union from coming to power, has certainly grown in Central Europe since the suppression of the Hungarian uprising. It is, however, to be doubted that there is any genuine loyalty or enthusiasm for the satellite Communist regimes or any radical decrease in the underlying hatred of them on the part of the mass of the people and the intellectuals. It is, therefore, highly doubtful that the U.S.S.R. would, even today, accept any form of agreement which would, in fact, result in the withdrawal of Soviet forces behind the boundaries of the U.S.S.R.

Even if it could be demonstrated that the U.S.S.R. would not possibly accept any agreement which entailed the complete withdrawal of its military forces from Central Europe, it can be argued that the West should put forward such a proposal merely for the political and propaganda effects of advocating it. I believe the argument on the other side—that the effect of putting forward such proposals would be more unsettling to the West than to the East— deserves consideration.

A further issue arises as to whether a buffer zone created by the withdrawal of the military forces of the major powers really would contribute to a continuing reduction of tensions and of the danger of war. It has frequently been pointed out that the withdrawal of United States military forces from South Korea did not prevent war breaking out there. An area of unsettled political control, a so-called power vacuum, is more apt to result in conflict and in war than is the direct confrontation across an established boundary of the military forces of opposed major powers. More basic political issues than mere distance between opposed forces should be settled if a program of disengagement is to have any lasting effect. If the intervening area is recognized by both sides to fall within the power sphere of one or the other, the disengagement is apt to result in decreased rather than increased possibilities of friction and of war. In 1948 it was our purpose that the intervening area would come to be governed by regimes responsive to the will of the peoples of Eastern Europe—in other words, that it would be in the power zone of the free world—even if it were militarily neutral. If the Soviets had indicated a willingness to withdraw their troops at that time, we would have interpreted it to mean that they accepted such a political solution to the problem of Eastern Europe. Today an evacuation of United States troops from Germany or from Europe would probably be interpreted by the Soviet Union, and by many Europeans, as acceptance by the West that all of continental Europe was thereafter to lie basically in the power sphere of the U.S.S.R. The U.S.S.R. for many years might well make no very direct demands upon the individual European nations, but the essential question of who is to decide the most basic issues—those potentially involving war or peace in the area—would, in their view, have been decided. The situation of Europe would then be comparable to the present position of Finland.

It can be argued, as George Kennan has argued, that Europe is in no condition to face another major war—be it a nuclear war or a war fought merely with conventional weapons—and that those things which are generally considered by students of defense matters to be necessary if there is to be an effective and credible deterrent to Soviet attack are either too costly and ignominious to be seriously considered, or more apt to invite an attack than to deter one. If one accepts this analysis, the U.S.S.R. is already in a position in which it can decide the basic issues of Europe—those involving a decision on peace or war in the area. In logic, it would then clearly follow that nothing essential would be risked by disengagement. An agreement to disengage would merely reflect the true power situation which had already been created by other factors. It would decrease the risk of war arising from a misunderstanding of those more basic power relationships.

Concerning this basic issue, NATO and its functions are of secondary importance. In 1948, we were not concerned with German membership in NATO or with the presence of substantial American ground forces on the Continent. The United States atomic monopoly seemed to satisfy the basic military strategic requirement. The withdrawal of Soviet military forces behind the Bug would give an opportunity for the inherent political forces within the area to find a more normal and hopeful mode of expression. Formal organizational instrumentalities such as

NATO seemed to be of secondary importance. Looking at today's very different situation, it can still be argued that the formal organizational instrumentalities should not be a bar to whatever may be wise from the standpoint of policy. If it were to be assumed that the U.S.S.R. would today accept an agreement under which the military forces of the U.S.S.R. would withdraw behind the Bug, that German reunification would then follow in some manner not wholly artificial and Communist-bound, and that the U.S.S.R. could reasonably be expected to live with such developments for an extended period of time because of purely political restraints upon her doing otherwise, then it would be intelligent to work out alternative organizational arrangements which would not impede such an agreement. This is merely to say that organizational arrangements such as NATO should not stand in the way of an agreement which would have the effect of permanently rolling back the U.S.S.R. from its unnatural position in the heart of Europe.

Thus two lines of approach have been advanced to justify disengagement. One is that the NATO countries are militarily so weak and so incapable of remedying their weakness that any attempt to persist in the present confrontation is apt to lead to a hopeless war, a war brought on by a miscalculation on our part as to the realities of the power situation. The other argument is that disengagement will result in great political victories for the West. These are assumed to include withdrawal of the Soviet Union from the heart of Europe, the reunification of Germany, and the growth within Central Europe of governments and economic institutions which, though they might differ substantially in form from American institutions, would be responsive to the will of the people in the area. These two approaches would appear at first view to be inconsistent. In George Kennan's analysis they become consistent because of the very great importance which he gives to political factors relative to military factors. In his opinion, twelve German divisions, backed by the general political restraints upon the U.S.S.R. against its bringing its superior military capabilities to bear, are adequate to give Germany a high degree of security; and the attempt to achieve a greater degree of security involves an excessive United States presence in Europe, an excessive reliance upon nuclear defenses, and a dangerous freezing of the present line across Europe.

The relative importance of political and military factors is not easy to define. Few students of the matter would deny the priority of political considerations over military. That relative military capabilities are an important component of the overall political situation, however, is hardly to be denied. In 1939, and again in 1950, the West rightly regretted that it had not paid more attention to this component in the preceding years of relative peace. Today it may well be true that we are putting excessive reliance upon nuclear armaments. But to agree to this is not to say that a favorable political future for Europe and for the West is to be foreseen if we concede to the U.S.S.R. a commanding and unchallengeable military position with respect to Europe.

Let us not attempt to relate our discussion of disengagement to our preceding discussion of alternatives to NATO. The point which seems to come out most clearly is that NATO is not an end in itself but an instrumentality in support of a particular line of policy. If one is persuaded that a radical change in policy is advisable, then radical alternatives to NATO may be in order. If one believes that political restraints against the U.S.S.R. using a preponderant military position can be relied upon, then there is little point in drawing lines and guaranteeing them by multilateral treaty arrangements. The presence of United States forces in Europe is then unnecessary. European forces can be adequate to deter any minor probing attacks. A general restraint against the Soviet Union initiating nuclear war can be provided by Polaris and Minuteman systems. A new political symbol and organization that is less oriented toward military matters and perhaps less exclusive in its membership would then be desirable.

The question of whether such a radical change in policy is advisable rests, at least in part, on an assessment of fact. The crucial judgment concerns the reliance that one can put upon the leaders of the Soviet Union being restrained by non-military, non-NATO, political considerations. No one would deny that such considerations exist. The Soviet leaders would obviously prefer not to engage in military operations beyond the borders of the U.S.S.R. and would recognize the adverse reaction within Russia and beyond their borders of initiating such operations. Are these considerations strong enough, however, to supervene against other considerations which might tempt the Soviet leaders to exploit a position of unchallengeable military superiority? The evidence that they are is hardly sufficient to warrant placing upon it the principal reliance of Western policy.

IV

The varieties of disengagement may constitute the currently most interesting class of proposals implying an alternative to NATO. There are, however, other important classes. One such class includes the proposals which would lead to union, federation, or at least confederation within a given area and which would thereby supersede NATO or make it irrelevant.

Two separate strands of thought can be identified as lying behind these proposals. One strand is the thought that an excessive dedication to national interests leads to chauvinism, national rivalries, and international tensions; and that there is, therefore, virtue in any arrangement which will subordinate dedication to national sovereignty and national interests to loyalties to some much larger political entity. The other strand is the thought that very large and highly integrated political units are necessary to survival in today's world.

The most radical of the proposals advanced advocate world government or a United Nations so strengthened as to constitute a close approximation to world government.[*] These proposals raise two basic issues. The first is the question of how the power of decision and the power of enforcement of decisions are to be organized and who is conceived of as ending up with effective control of these powers. The second is the question of feasibility.

Most of the proposals for world government assume that the power of decision and of enforcement will be organized through democratic institutions roughly comparable to those which have evolved in the Western world, and that the effective control of these powers will be exercised by the peoples of the world in their own interest. The role of

---

[*]*There are other proposals for increasing our support of the United Nations which do not imply world government. These are discussed in Section V below.*

leadership and of political parties and the difficulty of conceiving of political parties operating effectively across regional and continental lines seem to be ignored. That the Communists would accede to any system which did not assure them of the prospect of exercising effective control over the processes of decision-making and of enforcement seems inconceivable. If this judgment is accepted, the proposals for world government become merely one expression of the policy that flows from the belief that international tensions and the risk of war are, in the world of the future, the supreme evils, and that even a world controlled by the Communists is preferable to a divided world.

The more modest proposals for union, federation, or confederation accept the prospect of a politically divided world and of the dangers of tension and of the war which are inherent in this prospect. The object of these proposals is to improve the unity and strength of the peoples in the area concerned rather than to eliminate tension with other areas. Again we have the question of how the power of decision and of enforcement are to be organized and the question of feasibility. We also have the further question as to whether closer union among a select group of free-world countries will strengthen or divide the free-world system as a whole.

The project which is furthest advanced and which most nearly meets the test of feasibility is the Community of Six. With respect to certain specific functions the institutions which have been created by the Community of Six go beyond the mere coordination of national policies. The agreements contemplate progress toward full political unity. It is yet to be seen, however, how the power over vital decisions such as those affecting Algeria or the reunification of Germany is to be organized and enforced and where the locus of effective power is to be. The French appear to believe that the locus of effective power will be in French leadership. The Germans and the Dutch hardly share that view.

At the present stage of development of the Community of Six, no question of an alternative to NATO arises. NATO continues to be necessary as an overall political and defense umbrella under which the evolution of the Community of Six can proceed.

In this context, the question of an alternative to NATO could in the future arise in one of two ways. The Six might come to believe that the risks and disadvantages of the United States connection outweigh its advantages, and that such cohesion and strength as they can develop among themselves must be their reliance for survival. The Six might be able to make it not worth the candle for the Soviet Union to attack them directly with military force. It is hardly conceivable, however, that by themselves they could carry much weight in major political issues in other parts of the world. The task of providing a balance to the Soviet system in world politics would then fall squarely on the shoulders of the United States, either alone or with the British Commonwealth.

The other way in which an alternative to NATO could arise in this context would be if the United States decided to withdraw its effective support from the Continent or from NATO as a whole. In that event, problems similar to those mentioned in the preceding paragraph would arise, though from the opposite cause.

It has been suggested that an independent strategic nuclear deterrent in the hands either of the individual continental European powers, or of the Community of Six, would significantly change the otherwise gloomy prospects of the above contingencies. It is doubtful, however, that the U.S.S.R. is going to be much deterred by nuclear systems which it could at any time eliminate by an initial strike of its own. To provide nuclear systems which could survive an initial Soviet strike is no easy or cheap task, particularly with limited geographic resources. Perhaps Polaris, Minuteman, or some yet undiscovered system will provide such a capability in the future. But, even then, the credibility may be low that such systems will in fact be used other than in reply to the utmost provocation—a provocation tantamount to the threat of national destruction. There is thus little prospect of escape from the necessity for a broad coalition including both Europe and the United States if the general power of the Soviet system is to remain balanced.

Projects for political union or confederation in areas greater than NATO or smaller than NATO, therefore, do not appear to offer much hope as feasible or effective alternatives to NATO.

V

One further class of possible alternatives to NATO deserves to be mentioned. This class of alternatives addresses itself to the question of the exclusiveness of the NATO club.

It can be argued that the principal threat to the free world is not that of military attack or military pressure against Europe. The more immediate threat is continuing economic and political pressure against the so-called "grey areas," backed by the growing general economic power and productivity of the U.S.S.R. From this point of view, continued emphasis upon NATO and its military problems is detrimental rather than helpful. To many in Asia, Africa, and even Latin America, NATO is an exclusive club of those who are predominantly of the white race, native to the Western culture, and highly industrialized. It is a club from which they are excluded and the existence of which impinges upon their prestige and their aspiration for an equal place in the sun. What is generally called anti-colonialism, now that colonialism is on the way to being liquidated in most areas of the world, can be more directly equated with resentment against this exclusiveness than with resentment against colonialism as such. It is directed as much against the United States as against those European countries that still maintain colonial possessions.

If one starts from this set of considerations, one is led to a search for institutional arrangements which are non-exclusive and in which the new and emerging nations of the grey areas can participate as equals, not necessarily in power and prestige, but in qualification for membership. The obvious institution is the United Nations. Many of the proponents of greater emphasis upon that organization do not have in mind transforming it into a world government. They have in mind a shift of United States emphasis from NATO, the exclusive institution, to the United Nations, the inclusive institution. They recognize the limitation which the Soviet veto in the Security Council places upon the effectiveness of the United Nations as a decision-making organ. However, they believe that that limitation is overbalanced by the fact that the United Nations can have a positive influence in the areas that are most directly threatened, while the influence of the NATO powers, insofar as they act through NATO, will in these areas be negative. The NATO powers acting as NATO powers in the Middle East, for instance, can only succeed in generating antagonisms.

Only in its most extreme form does this line of thought suggest an alternative to—or rather the liquidation of—NATO. Under this proposal the essential functions of NATO could be dealt with in the following manner. The Charter of the United Nations gives guarantees against the use of military forces across national borders. The individual NATO nations could re-emphasize their determination to live up to their commitment to the Charter if the boundaries of the NATO nations, or the boundaries of other members of the United Nations, were breached by military force. They could deploy such military forces as might be necessary to demonstrate their will and ability to live up to these commitments pursuant to bilateral arrangements with the countries concerned. The coordination of policy could take place through normal diplomatic channels. The principal overt force of Western policy would be directed to building political and economic strength where it was really needed, in the threatened grey areas of the world.

Another proposal along the same general line is that there be negotiated a general Article 51 pact in which all the nations considering themselves threatened by military aggression might participate. This again would be non-exclusive as between North Atlantic and grey-area countries. The emphasis, however, would be on defense against military aggression, while the former proposal places the emphasis upon defense against economic and political pressure.

Both of these proposals meet with a cool reception among European countries. It is even doubtful whether in the current climate of opinion the more radical alternatives which flow from this line of thought would find acceptance in Asia or in Africa. The issue of relative emphasis to be placed upon meeting the threat of military aggression in Europe or of dealing with political and economic pressure in the grey areas is, however, a very real issue indeed.

VI

If we think back over the various alternatives to NATO which we have discussed and consider the grounds which are advanced in support of and in opposition to them, a number of points seem to emerge.

The way in which the threat to the free world's security is evaluated and the line of policy advocated obviously bear a relationship to each other. The interesting question is the nature of the causal connection between the two. Sometimes one has the impression that those advocating a line of policy evaluate the nature of the threat, not on the basis of such objective evidence as exists, but in terms that support the line of policy which they find most congenial. Those interested in the economic development of the underdeveloped areas tend to see the threat largely in economic terms, while those interested in military policy tend to see it largely in military terms. Evaluation of the threat, in logic, should be an operation independent of the policy preferences of the evaluator. On the other hand, policy is not merely a reaction to a threat. It is in part a constructive process independent of the nature of the threat. The difficulty is in keeping the various considerations that bear on policy sufficiently distinct from each other so that policy can be analyzed with some degree of rationality.

Judgment as to whether an alternative to NATO should be pursued depends in part, then, on as objective as possible an evaluation of the threat. If the facts justify a judgment that the threat is almost solely economic and political, some radical alternative to NATO would be in order. If the facts justify a further judgment that the threat is primarily directed against the Asian-African countries and not against Europe, the range of alternatives is further narrowed. If the facts justify the reverse of these judgments, only those alternatives which would increase the military strength and cohesion of the Atlantic countries would seem in order. If, however, the facts support the more usual evaluation that the threat is complex, covering all fronts and all modes of attack, including the possibility of a military threat to Europe, then the question becomes one not of an alternative to NATO, but of the proper place of NATO within a much broader structure of policy which includes as one of its parts the military defense of Europe.

More difficult to analyze is the proper weight to be given to efforts to strengthen the West in its adversary relationship with the Soviet-Chinese-Communist world and the weight to be given to surmounting or mitigating that relationship. Here we not only need a judgment of the threat and a sense of the thrust of our own purpose, but we must also judge the feasibility of meeting the threat, on the other hand, and of mitigating the adversary relationship, on the other. The question of feasibility continually recurs in choosing between longer-range policies. In the short run, most policies which differ substantially from current policy appear to be infeasible and generally are. But where policy modifications have as their object effects to be achieved over a number of years, the evidence of experience is that much more can generally be done than at first seems possible.

In conclusion, it may be appropriate to re-emphasize the obvious point that consideration of alternatives to NATO is merely another way of considering the alternatives to overall Western policy.

14. The United States Defense Policy and NATO*

(1962)

This afternoon I propose to discuss with you four principal themes: First, the reliance of the United States upon the North Atlantic Treaty Organization as the central element in the common defense of an interdependent North America and Western Europe; second, the rationale for the U.S. emphasis upon a non-nuclear military buildup concurrently with a further strengthening of the West's

---

*Soon after taking office in 1961, President John F. Kennedy ordered a reappraisal of U.S. and allied defense requirements, with special emphasis, as Nitze had long advocated, on reducing NATO's reliance on nuclear weapons by increasing conventional strength. What emerged was the strategy of "flexible response" to replace the Eisenhower administration's outmoded policy of massive retaliation. At first, the European allies greeted the proposed change of strategy with considerable skepticism, some accusing the United States that it no longer took European security seriously enough to risk nuclear war. As assistant secretary of defense for international security affairs and a principal architect of the flexible response doctrine, it fell upon Nitze to explain the new strategy in a manner persuasive to the West Germans, whose interests were most directly involved. The result was this speech to the Amerika-Gesellschaft in Hamburg on April 11, 1962. Though Nitze delivered the speech in German, it is reprinted here in its official English translation.

nuclear deterrent; third, the progress of current U.S. and NATO efforts to build greater military capability for both the Berlin crisis and the long-term strength of the Alliance; and fourth, some personal reflections about the future evolution of NATO and the Atlantic Community to reflect both the indivisibility of the defense of Europe and North America as well as the new strength of the European members of the Alliance.

As you all know, we in America have watched with keen and sympathetic interest the evolution of Western Europe from the post World War II devastation through reconstruction with the assistance of our Marshall Plan aid, on to the Coal and Steel Community, the European Common Market and Euratom, and today's efforts toward closer political bonds with each other. Concurrent with the growth of this stronger and closer European community has been the growth of the Atlantic Community. These trends toward an Atlantic Community are founded on many common cultural, historical and political ties, and economic interests. Today, as a result of the existence and growing military strength of the Communist bloc, the need for greater unity within the Western community and between Western Europe and North America in matters of defense is manifest. In fact, modern technology and its effects on the time and space factors in strategic planning have made anachronistic the idea that the members of the Atlantic Community can continue to plan for their defense on an individual national basis in the tradition of the 19th century. Today the defense of Europe and North American is indivisible. NATO, of course, sprang from recognition of our common defense interests and is one of the best examples of the vitality of our common civilization in meeting new challenges in the world.

The impetus for NATO is found in the Communist ideology which calls for the worldwide triumph of "socialism." Their new dogma calls for this to be done through the techniques of so-called "peaceful coexistence," which includes "just wars," or "wars of liberation." The extraordinary perversion of language in which totalitarian Communist regimes style themselves as "democracies" and label our Western defense measures as "aggression" confuses the issue for many people. To the Communists, "peace" constitutes a state of affairs in which they gain domination without open warfare. Under their inverted logic, the only danger to "peace" is from those who propose to stand firm against their aggression—those who would risk war rather than surrender under external aggressive pressure the values of the society of their choice. General Karl von Clausewitz recognized many years ago that an aggressor is always peace-loving, for he wants to acquire the territory of his victim unopposed. Clausewitz pointed out that war exists for the benefit of the defender; war results from a defender's willingness to fight for his vital interests rather than surrender them in the face of aggression.

The growth of Soviet military power, coupled with centralized direction of at least the European part of the bloc and guided by the foregoing ideology, faces the Atlantic Community with one of its great tests. NATO is our central response to this test.

A succession of U.S. presidents has consistently recognized NATO's importance. When the new Democratic administration came into office about fifteen months ago, President Kennedy immediately ordered a reappraisal of our defense requirements, including our strategic plans and the nuclear and non-nuclear capabilities of our forces. The continuance of an overriding U.S. concern with the security of Europe and the strengthening of the NATO alliance was one of the first and most important results of this reappraisal. President Kennedy, last spring, reaffirmed our commitments to Europe's security and our intention to maintain the strength of our forces here.

This re-examination also reflected our belief that the NATO relationship had changed from the days of its creation in 1948 when the significant effect of the alliance was the commitment of U.S. power to the support of Europe. Since then, NATO has evolved from this primary reliance on U.S. power to one of substantial inter-dependence—in military as in other aspects—between the European and American partners. This is natural. First, just as it is not practical for Western Europe to develop the entire range of military forces—nuclear as well as non-nuclear—to offset fully the Soviet military threat, it is not practical for the U.S. to achieve military self-sufficiency independent of NATO. Second, the astonishing economic success of Western Europe in the last decade, in addition to reaffirming the vitality of Western civilizations as a whole, has justified a more equal sharing of the economic burden of the common Western defense. Third, increased European political unity and political strength carries with it increased European responsibilities to NATO. As your defense minister, Herr Strauss, put it in his Nash memorial lecture at Georgetown University last November: "The former one way street becomes one where traffic moves in both directions."

Such was the general context in which the new administration reviewed its initial defense policies. The immediate and operative decisions for us in the Defense Department inevitably dealt with questions of men, money, and equipment. Policy, of course, is not only the guide to but is also importantly affected by such practical decisions. Behind these decisions are to be found analysis and choice.

Reflecting our worldwide responsibilities, we recognized three basic types of military challenge which our defense establishment should be designed to deter if possible and fight if necessary: nuclear war; non-nuclear combat; and covert aggression—ranging from subversion to guerrilla warfare to outright insurgency.

Our efforts have been directed to meeting all three of these threats. There has been general understanding and acceptance of the rationale and importance of the first and third efforts. The justification for the non-nuclear buildup and its relation to the defense of the central front in NATO has not been as well understood.

As my second principal theme, I would like to suggest a justification for the emphasis the U.S. has placed on bringing NATO's non-nuclear capability into better balance with the nuclear forces. I realize that some people regard the non-nuclear buildup as irrelevant in a world where nuclear weapons are at the disposal of each of the two major groups of powers facing each other across the iron curtain. They argue, for example, that *any* clash of arms will inevitably and immediately escalate to general nuclear war and that the buildup of NATO's non-nuclear forces is defeatist, divisive, and undermines the credibility to the Soviets of our nuclear deterrent. I disagree with these judgments. I believe that the non-nuclear buildup materially enhances the credibility of our deterrent. Furthermore, in its own right it gives us the means directly to counter, and thus to deter, certain important options which otherwise would be available to the Communists. Finally, it is a prerequisite for a true "forward strategy" for the defense of

Europe, a strategy designed to meet any Communist attack at the borders—not after they have been penetrated.

Consider what capabilities, what statements and what courses of action on our part are likely to affect the Soviet Union's judgment on whether aggressive courses of action on its part will be likely to bring it unacceptably close to the danger of nuclear war.

I should think the most persuasive capability would be the Western nuclear arsenal, its capacity to survive anything Soviet forces can do, its capacity to penetrate Soviet defenses, its responsiveness to responsible control, and its accuracy, numbers, and power.   On this score, as I shall point out in a few minutes, the facts support a very credible deterrent indeed.

A second factor is the indications the Soviets get from Western words and statements as to what the West regards as interests which it is determined to protect.   Western leaders have already declared in clear and unambiguous words our joint determination to defend Western interests in Berlin.

The third factor is that of action.   What are the actions through which we can convincingly demonstrate that aggression against our interests, if persisted in, will thereby create a situation in which the danger of nuclear war is very great indeed?   Let us assume two hypothetical situations.

In the first hypothetical situation, the central NATO front is very lightly covered by our forces. It is subject to the risk of deep penetration by Soviet non-nuclear forces stationed opposite to those of NATO. In this situation the only option for military action open to the West, in the event of even a minor Soviet challenge, is an immediate nuclear response.

In the second hypothetical situation, the NATO front is firmly held on a continuous line pursuant to a "forward strategy." There are enough NATO forces to mount a really serious non-nuclear probe in the air corridors or along the autobahn in the event of Soviet actions against Western interests in Berlin. That probe can be thrown back only by the massive application of Soviet power in a major fight against NATO forces, which in turn would surely bring on a Western nuclear response.

If you were on the other side, which of these two hypothetical situations would you consider more laden with a risk of nuclear war? In which would you be more inclined to refrain from a series of actions designed, step by step, to erode the West's interests? To me, the answer is clear. I would consider it much more evident that the West would find it politically possible to act effectively in defense of its interests from the second posture than from the first.

The difficulty with the first hypothetical situation is that it simply is not credible that we or anyone else will respond to a given small step with the immediate use of nuclear weapons.

Some opponents of the non-nuclear buildup fear that as we build our strength, we will be tempted to rely exclusively on non-nuclear forces if Communist forces penetrate the NATO area. This fear is unjustified. In case of a massive conventional attack which would put any significant portion of NATO territory in danger of being overrun, the West would have to respond with all available means. This includes nuclear weapons.

These considerations apply with particular force to the current situation with respect to Berlin. The continued freedom of Berlin has more importance to the West than the suppression of that freedom has to the Communists. We must have the means of bringing this fact home to them by action as well as by words, and thus impress upon them a realization of full danger they would incur in pushing their campaign against the integrity of Berlin—the danger that they will bring upon themselves an irreversible situation.

This leads to my third theme: the growing overall military strength of the NATO alliance. Part of this growing NATO strength results from actions we have taken in the United States. As soon as it took office, the new Kennedy administration decided that one of its first tasks was to assure that the United States would be in a position to play its full part in meeting both the nuclear and the non-nuclear threats to the West. The practical problems were those of force structure, procurement, research and development, and training.

The first half of the U.S. effort has been to improve the quality of our nuclear deterrent, its capacity to survive a surprise attack, and its ready responsiveness to command and control. The other half of our effort has been to raise substantially the level of our non-nuclear capabilities. We have already made solid progress in both areas.

The efforts we have made in the nuclear area convince us that we are today fully capable of destroying any target system of our choice even after absorbing an initial nuclear surprise attack. Since President Kennedy took office, we have expanded the existing program for the construction of Polaris submarines to an eventual total of 41, and accelerated planned deliveries so that the 12th to 29th submarines will be delivered at the rate of one a month, and the 30th to 41st at the rate of two a month. We already have had over 125,000 man-days of "on station" experience with the Polaris submarine. The program for an initial twelve squadrons totaling 600 hardened and dispersed solid fuel Minuteman strategic missiles is under way. We already plan to add an additional four, and probably more, squadrons later. We have augmented the funds to be applied to the development of Skybolt. To protect our bomber forces from destruction in surprise attack we have increased our ground and airborne alert capacities and have improved our air defense and warning systems. We are pursuing research and development of an AICBM. What has been, perhaps, most significant for the short-term future is that it has proved possible to bring 50 percent of our manned bomber force to a 15 minute ground alert status.

We have also carefully examined the organization and technical aspects of command and control of the strategic deterrent so that the proper political authority can at all times personally exercise positive control over the commitment of nuclear weapons.

Now that the problems of survivability and of command and control are becoming manageable, we believe that the overall nuclear forces available to the West, including the NATO nuclear forces deployed on the Continent, give us a definite nuclear advantage over the U.S.S.R. in purely military terms. We further believe this military advantage can be maintained in the future, as improved weapon systems are developed and deployed by both sides. This military advantage is of central importance in the equations of deterrence and political strategy.

The other half of the new administration's initial defense program was to strengthen our non-nuclear strength to help deter general war and to meet non-nuclear aggression. Here again, and particularly under the impetus of the serious tension over Berlin, we have made solid progress. The President selected three specific areas for improvements: a higher priority for research; development and production of non-nuclear weapons; an increased flexibility of non-nuclear forces including air lift and sea lift capacity; and increased personnel and training for combatting covert aggression. We have augmented the 11 permanent U.S. Army combat-ready divisions available last July by about 45 percent to a total of 16 combat-ready divisions. We have also made major improvements in our tactical air, our naval capabilities, and in support and logistics forces.

These concrete improvements in U.S. non-nuclear capabilities have been complemented by a concurrent series of actions by our NATO allies. The Federal Republic of Germany has been a leader in this buildup, having provided nine NATO divisions by the end of 1961 and taken the measures which promise an additional two divisions by the end of 1962. Canada, France, and the Netherlands have also made responses worthy of particular note.

For years NATO has fallen short of its firm and agreed non-nuclear force requirements. On the crucial central front that requirement has been approximately 30 M-day divisions. Last year we had about 21 divisions—many not being up to standard. By virtue of the actions we have taken together since then, effective NATO M-day divisions have been increased by more than 25 percent. This includes five fully manned and ready U.S. divisions and their supporting forces. If the situation makes it advisable, the U.S. contribution can be augmented on short notice by six additional divisions, the equipment for some of which has already been prepositioned in Europe. Beyond that are second echelon divisions.

It is our view that, as a minimum, NATO should have in being in the Central Region its full requirement of 30 M-day divisions, all excellently equipped and trained and with adequate, sensible combat and logistic support. We further believe that reserve forces should be augmented and should be well-equipped, well-manned, well-trained, and ready for early use in combat.

We also recognize that greater interdependence in NATO in the nuclear field is desirable. We strongly prefer a multilateral solution to this problem as against any proliferation of national nuclear capabilities.

Up to this point in my remarks I have dealt largely with the practical defense questions which have engaged us in the United States since January 1961 and have engaged NATO as a whole with particular force since the renewal last April of serious Communist threats to Berlin. As one looks back over this period I believe we have, on balance, done well. The NATO alliance is stronger today than it was a year ago. NATO's military posture is substantially improved. But only the future will reveal whether we have done well enough. Much depends on how we use the additional time which the actions of this last year have given us.

As we look to the future it is important to discuss frankly and forthrightly our varying conceptions of the future development of the Atlantic Community and the NATO alliance. To my mind the central issue here is how we each view our national interests in relation to the interests of the community as a whole.

There has been an important evolution of the United States' ideas on this subject. I believe the crucial turning point in United States post-war foreign policy took place in the short space of twenty weeks in the spring of 1947. That twenty-week period began in April with the Truman Doctrine, announcing United States willingness to lend its support to all countries themselves prepared to fight in defense of their national independence from Communist aggression. It continued with the Greek-Turkish assistance program. It included ratification of the Act of Chapultepec by the Rio Pact which ended the long American tradition against what we previously called entangling alliances. Those same twenty weeks saw the passage of the National Security Act of 1947 which created the department with which I now serve as part of a comprehensive set of organizations to deal with our national security policy. That period also included the creation within the State Department of the Policy Planning Staff with which I formerly served. The culminating act of this period of intense activity was Secretary of State Marshall's speech proposing for the consideration of Europe the now famous European Recovery Plan.

The significant point about this twenty week period was that it marked a national decision by the United States on the crucial issue of interdependence. We had come to the firm conclusion as a nation that our well being and security could no longer be pursued in isolation from others or by merely intermittent involvement in the affairs of the world. We had decided that our security and well being could only be fostered in the larger context of the Atlantic Community acting in harmony with the interests of the non-Communist world as a whole. Furthermore, those twenty weeks demonstrated that we were prepared to act promptly and comprehensively in support of that decision.

Dramatic changes have occurred in the subsequent fifteen years. The economic recovery of Europe has succeeded beyond anyone's most hopeful anticipations. A host of new nations has come to sovereignty; and colonialism has become a residual issue. The Soviet Union has developed a large and threatening nuclear capability. The mainland of China has come under Communist control. The interdependence of the non-Communist nations has taken on new dimensions, enhancing our need for cooperation.

As one looks into the future, what should be the form and nature of interdependence in Europe and in the Atlantic Community? Should the answer be the same in the political field, in the economic field, and in the defense field? How can the various considerations best complement each other? There are national, European, and Atlantic considerations as well as functional ones such as the economic and the military. What organizational arrangements should flow from the decisions reached? All these matters are under intensive debate throughout the Atlantic Community. It is obviously too early to express any authoritative views.

I should, however, like to put forward certain purely personal observations. In large measure they will be restatements of the obvious, of ideas which are widely shared, certainly by you who are in this audience.

The first of these is that it continues to be true for all of us on both sides of the Atlantic that our well being and security are to be found not in the pursuit of purely national interests but in the wider Atlantic context.

There undoubtedly can be, and are, differing views as to what specific actions are, or are not, in the interest of the community as a whole. We in the United States claim no precedence in wisdom on such matters. We do, however, believe it proper to insist that the context in which the judgments are made is the broader alliance context, and not primarily a national one.

The second point I should like to make is that the political, economic, and military spheres are so interconnected that what is done in one sphere is bound to have consequences in each of the others. The growing economic integration of Europe draws Europe closer to political integration, and this in turn may have consequences for the defense arrangements within NATO. Similarly it is appropriate to point out that the defense requirements of the alliance can and should have their influence on the form which the economic and political evolution of the alliance takes. Defense requirements permit, and I believe call for, close collaboration in the formulation of the alliance's defense program and in the development of its policies. They call for unity and decisiveness of command if and when alliance forces must actually be used. And finally I believe they require the full resources of the alliance. A federated Europe would obviously simplify many of our current NATO defense problems. It would not, however, permit Europe and North America to diminish the defense ties that bind together the two sides of the Atlantic. It is my view that the primary organ of coordination in defense matters should be NATO. Problems such as those suggested by the figure of fifteen fingers upon a safety catch, or upon a trigger are made no easier by dividing each such problem into two concurrent problems.

But progress toward greater interdependence cannot always proceed with equal speed in all spheres or in all areas of the Atlantic Community. The important point is that it is proceeding with good will and with attention to the main issues.

I have outlined for you several major features of current U.S. defense policy. First, NATO is central to the U.S. defense and national security objectives in much the same way as the U.S. is central to the defense and national security concerns of the other NATO powers. We are interdependent in an indivisible task. Second, we believe that increases in non-nuclear forces substantially enhance the credibility of the alliance's nuclear deterrent, and improve its military power. Third, the U.S. is building a stronger nuclear force as well as participating in the NATO buildup of a stronger non-nuclear capability. Finally, I have put forward some personal ideas on future developments within the Atlantic Community.

The actions which the U.S. has taken in the course of the present Berlin situation amply demonstrate the fullness of my country's commitment to the defense of Europe. That commitment has never been more universally accepted in the U.S. than it is today.

We in the United States strongly believe that NATO's political as well as its military problems are moving toward a favorable solution as all of us on both sides of the Atlantic work and sacrifice together toward a common goal. That goal is rooted in our mutual defense but it encompasses something bigger: our shared beliefs in the freedom and democratic institutions which characterize Western civilization.

"The United States Defense Policy and NATO" is reprinted from *Public Statements of Assistant Secretary of Defense for International Security Affairs, Paul H. Nitze, 1961-1963*, vol. 1 (Washington: Department of Defense, n.d.), pp. 112-134.

15. What Bush Should Do To Solve
The NATO Flap*

(1989)

From the early days of NATO 40 years ago, it has often been charged that NATO was an alliance in disarray. And often the charge appeared to be well-founded, particularly when General Charles de Gaulle withdrew France from the NATO military organization (though not from the North Atlantic Treaty). But these differences, though serious, could in time be worked out and did not result in a shattering of the alliance.

Today's controversy with the German government concerning negotiations with the Soviets on "short-range nuclear missiles" could be much more serious. The continental European countries are backing Germany against the Anglo-Saxons—President Bush and Secretary of State James A. Baker III, prodded by an adamant British Prime Minister Margaret Thatcher.

There has long been a tension in U.S. policy toward Europe between the special relationship between England and America developed by Churchill and Roosevelt during World War II and the fact that the sector crucial to the defense of NATO is the central front on the continent of Europe. Partially as a result of the latter fact, Germany

---

*Mr. Nitze wrote this article at the request of the Washington Post at the time of the debate within NATO and the U.S. government on the short range missiles located in West Germany.

and France have been at the heart of our European policy during the post-war years.

When England and the United States join in hectoring demands for action by the continental NATO countries, this is taken as unwarranted pressure by the Anglo-Saxons, who are not viewed by the continentals as being true Europeans. Furthermore, the uncompromising position of the Anglo-Saxons against any negotiations with the Soviets about short-range missiles—while concurrently demanding that West Germany some time in the future agree to modernization of our Lance missiles in Germany—is politically unacceptable to the German government. The Germans are being backed by the other NATO continental European powers. Unless a compromise can be found, those relationships can split the alliance with the serious consequences to NATO unity that Gorbachev has long hoped would drop into his lap.

What should be done about all this? At the beginning of this administration, I outlined to Secretary of State Baker an approach that I thought could give us the initiative in working out a solution. My suggestion was that we talk to the West German government, specifically to Chancellor Helmut Kohl, and propose the following course of action:

Rather than refuse to negotiate with the Soviets on the subject of the zero-to-300-mile nuclear missiles deployed in Germany, I suggested that we tell Kohl we would be prepared to ask the Soviets to participate in such negotiations under certain conditions. The first condition would be that Kohl and his government agree to stick to their long-standing position that they are firmly opposed to the total elimination of short-range nuclear ballistic missiles; second, that his government back us in seeking equal ceilings with the Soviets on such missiles at a level substantially above zero (preferably in the 200- to 300-missile range); and thirdly, that NATO as a whole support this initiative.

I emphasized that the current U.S. position of insisting on German agreement to modernize Lance while adamantly refusing to consider negotiations with the Soviets on the subject could not today be agreed to by any conceivable German government.

It has been argued, principally by Henry Kissinger, that to enter into a negotiation with the Soviets will inevitably result in agreeing to their possible demand for the total elimination of short-range missiles in Germany. To enter into a negotiation does not mean that we have to concur in the other side's demands. We have had 20 years of experience in demonstrating the reverse. It is true that a segment of West German political opinion favors the unilateral dismantling of the short-range missiles on German soil and will continue to do so even if we enter into negotiations with the Soviets on the subject. But it is also true that a majority of Germans favor maintaining the alliance and remaining useful partners with the rest of NATO including the United States. It should be the objective of U.S. policy to assist that majority, through our conduct, to prevail over the more politically active opposition groups.

There is another dimension to this issue—the military dimension. The Soviets have a large number of short-range missile launchers; it is estimated that the number of their launchers capable of launching this type of missile is 1,400; by contrast, the United States is generally estimated to have about 88 such launchers. The Soviet launchers can launch a variety of missiles, some armed with high explosives, some with chemical weapons, some with nuclear weapons. (One estimate is that the Soviets can deploy some 3,000 such nuclear-armed missiles of a significantly longer range than our present Lance missiles.) And in the absence of any agreed limitation, the Soviets are in a position to increase their inventory to any level they may consider necessary. Is it really wise to allow the Soviets to retain an immense ratio of advantage in this category of weaponry?

(Gorbachev's offer last week to Secretary of State Baker to unilaterally reduce the number of Soviet short-range missiles by 284 will somewhat reduce the existing imbalance; but it does not negate the desirability of a negotiated equal solution to this problem.)

It is argued that a U.S. ability to initiate an exchange of nuclear weapons, however militarily ineffective, will add a necessary rung to the ladder of graduated nuclear deterrence. But is it not possible to use other nuclear weapons of any range desired, if all that is required is to be able to initiate a nuclear exchange? We have an inventory of such weapons of every conceivable range. The principal deterrent to war with the Soviet Union, including both conventional and nuclear war, must in the end rest on our diverse and survivable panoply of strategic forces.

Would not we and NATO be more secure with a low but equal ceiling on the short-range missiles of both sides? The Soviets may not agree to this, but why refuse negotiations aimed at such an outcome?

A further question has been raised by Senator Sam Nunn, Representative Les Aspin, and others concerning the timing of stabilizing conventional-force reductions relative to negotiation on the limitation of short-range nuclear missiles. They are correct in arguing that the principal reason NATO needs short-range nuclear weapons is the great superiority of Warsaw Pact conventional forces over NATO conventional forces. The argument over whether to negotiate reduced equal ceilings on short-range nuclear forces would disappear if Warsaw Pact and NATO conventional forces were reduced to equal levels. But if we were able to achieve agreement on equal levels of short-range nuclear missiles in Europe at about the level I suggest we aim at, I see no reason why we should deny ourselves the benefit of the one-sided Soviet reductions implied by such an outcome until we have achieved a more ambitious (and I believe more time-consuming) goal of conventional-force reductions.

Achieving "stabilizing reductions in conventional forces" is an important—I believe the most important—of NATO goals. We have spent years negotiating a mandate for such talks in the framework of the Helsinki process. Negotiations between NATO countries and the Warsaw Pact countries are about to begin. These negotiations are properly multilateral—not bilateral between Washington and Moscow. On the NATO side, most of the conventional forces are non-U.S. forces; it would be improper for us to take over the negotiations from our NATO allies; they would resent any such American action.

Multilateral negotiations historically have taken much time. The Soviets some months ago announced a target of significant unilateral conventional-force reductions. But those reductions, if carried out, would still have left the Soviet Union with a dangerous superiority in tanks, self-propelled artillery, and other important items. In Moscow last week during Baker's visit, Gorbachev announced a proposal for much deeper multilateral reductions in Europe.

Whether this opens a prospect for a prompt resolution of these difficult problems will require intense study by NATO.

Behind the short-range missile issue is the question of whether the Soviet Union has really changed its spots. Should we try to encourage what appears to be constructive change in the Soviet Union, or should we be cautious until we know more? Will Gorbachev survive as the unquestioned arbiter of political decisions in the Soviet Union? If so, what will his objectives be, and if not, what direction will the Soviet Union take?

I doubt that this set of questions presents us with a real issue. We can both be cautious, not letting down our guard, and at the same time explore with the Soviets whether they are prepared to negotiate agreements that would, on balance, be helpful to us and acceptable to Gorbachev. Caution and exploration of the possible are not necessarily contradictory aims.

"What Bush Should Do To Solve The NATO Flap" is reprinted from *The Washington Post* (May 14, 1989), p. C1.

APPENDIX I

Mr. Nitze's Career

On December 5, 1984, Paul Henry Nitze was asked to serve as a special adviser to the President and secretary of state on arms control matters. Ambassador Nitze had been head of the United States Delegation to the Intermediate-Range Nuclear Forces Negotiations with the Soviet Union, which convened on November 30, 1981, in Geneva, Switzerland.

During the preceding seven years, Mr. Nitze was a consultant on defense policy and international relations to various government departments and private industry firms. He was also chairman of the Advisory Council of the Johns Hopkins School of Advanced International Studies; a director on the boards of Aspen Skiing Corporation, Twentieth Century-Fox Film Corporation, Schroders, Inc., American Security and Trust Company, the Ethics and Public Policy Center, and the Atlantic Council of the United States; trustee emeritus of the Aspen Institute for Humanistic Studies and the George C. Marshall Research Foundation; and chairman of Policy Studies, Committee on the Present Danger.

In the spring of 1969 Mr. Nitze was appointed representative of the secretary of defense to the United States Delegation to the Strategic Arms Limitation Talks with the Soviet Union, a position he held until June 1974, at which time he resigned.

Mr. Nitze resigned from his duties as deputy secretary of defense on January 20, 1969, a position he had held since July 1, 1967, succeeding Cyrus R. Vance.

Mr. Nitze was serving as 57th secretary of the Navy when he was nominated by President Lyndon B. Johnson on June 10, 1967 to become deputy secretary of defense. He was confirmed by the United States Senate on June 29, 1967.

The President John F. Kennedy nominated Mr. Nitze to be secretary of the navy on October 14, 1963. At that time he was serving as assistant secretary of defense for international security affairs, having assumed that position on January 29, 1961. He began his duties as secretary of the navy on November 29, 1963.

Graduated *cum laude* in 1928 from Harvard University, Mr. Nitze subsequently joined the New York investment banking firm of Dillon Read and Company. In 1941 he left his position as vice president of that firm to become financial director of the Office of the Coordinator of Inter-American Affairs.

From 1942-1943 he was chief of the Metals and Minerals Branch of the Board of Economic Warfare, until named as director of Foreign Procurement and Development for the Foreign Economic Administration.

During the period 1944-1946 Mr. Nitze was vice chairman of the United States Strategic Bombing Survey. He was awarded the Medal of Merit by President Truman for service to the nation in this capacity.

For the next seven years he served with the Department of State, beginning in the position of deputy director of the Office of International Trade Policy. In 1948 he was named deputy to the assistant secretary of state for economic affairs. In August 1949 he became deputy director of the State Department's Policy Planning Staff, and director the following year.

Mr. Nitze left the federal government in 1953 to become president of the Foreign Service Educational Foundation in Washington, D.C., a position he held until January 1961.

Born in Amherst, Massachusetts on January 16, 1907, Mr. Nitze is married to the former Phyllis Pratt and has four children—Heidi, Peter, William, and Anina. Mr. Nitze maintains his legal residence in Washington, D.C., and has a residence in Bel Alton, Maryland.